THE AMERICAN MANIFESTO

A Critical Analysis of the American Cultural Psychology

A CONCERNED CITIZEN

Fulton Books, Inc.
Meadville, PA

Published by Fulton Books 2021

ISBN 978-1-63860-387-0 (paperback)
ISBN 978-1-63860-388-7 (digital)

Printed in the United States of America

If you're looking for the guilty, you need only look into a mirror.

—V

CONTENTS

INTRODUCTION

Insects will appear only after things are rotten.

—Su Shi

The inspiration for writing this book came from scholars and other thinkers throughout the Arab world. Such as Saudi Shura Council Member Ibrahim Al-Buleihi or Syrian Author Nidhal Naisa, who openly spoke out against the societal norms of the Arab world. Seeing their arguments made me begin to realize something, something I didn't like. And it compelled me to speak out against what I saw by writing this book.

It is known that the United States is suffering from a multitude of problems—coronavirus and a collapsing economy, just to name a few. Many others include gun violence, a healthcare crisis, collapsing infrastructure, police brutality, homelessness in inner cities, mass suicide amongst veterans, missing and murdered Indigenous women, missing and murdered transgender women, a failing education system, rising costs of living, student loan crisis, massive wealth inequality, corruption, and all of this occurring under the ever-larger presence of climate change.

And as the American people grapple with this, outsiders are noticing and taking advantage. As I write this, the Chinese are using economic soft power all over the world, gaining footholds in Europe, Africa, the Middle East, Central Asia, Australia, and Oceania. Only the United States and India seem to be exempt from this ever-encroaching Chinese influence.

But of course, the question ultimately remains, why? Why is it that the United States still has this problem? Why have the American people and their government not come together and fix these problems? And why is it that so many Americans would rather slide these issues to the sidelines rather than tackle them head-on?

It is very easy to write all of this off as being special interests and Wall Street donors. But the purpose of writing this book is to not say that special interests and Wall Street donors are not a problem. But it would be a waste of time, a waste of paper, and a waste of ink to just reiterate things that everyone else has already said because this alone does not explain the rise of Donald Trump. No, the purpose of writing this book is to bring attention to something else.

Much like the dissidents in the Arab world sounding the alarm, American culture is very fundamentally flawed. And so through these various chapters, I shall explain to you what is wrong with American cultural values and American societal norms. The point of view will be from someone who is outside the United States looking in. It is always a thing for politicians in Washington DC to say, "We need to lead with American values," but what are those values? What if these "American values" that Americans cherish are fundamentally in the wrong? Every world dictator, from Pol Pot to Mao Zedong to Joseph Stalin to Adolf Hitler has used the phrase, "We have to lead with our values," to justify horrific atrocities. Just because they are your values doesn't mean that they are therefore good.

Nor is anything that I am about to say revolutionary or anything that hasn't been tried before. What I am about to say was already done by the Germans, following the Second World War. In looking for an answer to the question as to how it was that Hitler was able to come to power, the Germans began to reexamine German cultural norms and from the perspective that they were non-Germans looking at Germany from the outside. What they found was that German culture was rotten to its core. And if Americans did an honest analysis of themselves, I think that they will find that American culture, American values, are rotten to their core.

But what exactly was it that the Germans found? It is very easy to put the rise of Hitler as being centered on German bitterness, following their defeat in the First World War, the one-sidedness of the Treaty of Versailles, the hyperinflation of the Weimar Republic, and the Great Depression. But it doesn't quite explain the Aryan master race theory. Indeed, the Germans realized that Hitler would not have been possible without the militaristic culture that had defined the German identity since Fredrick the Great made Prussia a major European power during the Austrian War of Succession. And it, too, does not explain the Holocaust. After all, a society, that was supposedly tolerant of Jews, Gypsies, homosexuals, and others before the Nazis came to power, could not have overnight agreed with the anti-Semitic and antiziganist being spewed by the Nazi Party and become complicit in the deaths of eleven million people.

Indeed, if the American people, who at least a good chunk of them, truly are terrified by the actions of Donald Trump and never want anyone like him to ever return to power again, Americans must examine the conditions that led to him coming to power in the first place and not just the socioeconomic conditions; the Rust Belt to inner cities and American cultural values and ask if the faults of American culture are showing in the form of Donald Trump.

But as I said, a good chunk. A good chunk are Trump cultists who have created their own little version of Jonestown, Guyana, or Waco, Texas. Indeed, many people reading this will feel offended and clutch their pearls. It is because of this that I, at least for now, have chosen to write this under a pen name but may in the future reveal my true identity.

The basic message which is so horrific is, that as I have stated before, the fundamentals of the American cultural mindset. Mainly being, like the message that the Arab dissidents Ibrahim Al-Buleihi, Nidhal Naisa, and others, Americans are backward. What's more, many Americans are not even aware of how backward they are. And Americans are, therefore, nowhere near breaking free of their backwardness because Americans must first acknowledge that they are backward. Over the next several chapters, I shall explain in detail the backwardness of American ideology. It is in the hopes that people who read this heed my warnings and work to change America's mindset. And once America has rid herself of her backwardness, future generations, when reading this, will look on in horror that this was the cultural psychology that Americans believed. And that they will do everything in their power to ensure that such backward thinking never reoccur again.

And so, in this first chapter, I shall explain the origin of America's backwardness, to explain how we got to where we are now.

CHAPTER 1

On the Origins of the American Mindset

Western belief in the universality of Western culture suffers three problems: it is false, it is immoral, and it is dangerous.

—Samuel Huntington

I am going to begin this discussion with geography. Geography has shaped cultures throughout history. The United States is no exception.

The United States is one of the most blessed geographies on earth. Bordered by two oceans, the heartland further nestled in by two mountains, full of vast riverways, and a natural wall of islands that bear the brunt of severe storms before it moves inland. America can afford to rest easy. The United States will never have to worry about an invasion. It does not build artificial walls to keep out hurricane damage because it does not need to. The islands do that job for them. It does not invest in agricultural machinery to boost productivity because it does not need to. The arable lands are vast enough on their own. In addition, there are vast reserves of coal, oil, natural gas, gold, and silver. All of this causes the United States to develop a vast labor pool and become, without lifting much of a figure, the richest and most powerful nations on earth. Only China has a similar blessing in its geography.

And because of that, American culture fell into the same trap that China fell into. A culture of conservatism and complacency set in. With everything they wanted at their doorstep and everyone looking to them for everything, the Chinese sat back, got lazy, and never modernized their country. The legacy of this conservatism is that Mandarin is still written in a series of pictographs rather than an alphabet system.

This lack to progress and advance ultimately came to haunt the country, when, after cracking down on opium trade that was forced upon them by the British in order to balance the trade deficit of the East India Company, the superior British navy decisively defeated the inferior Chinese navy. Starting of what became known to the Chinese as the "century of humiliation." Over time, more and more of China began to be chiseled out by foreign powers. But the leadership did not change. Society had become so enveloped into a culture of conservatism and complacency that they couldn't get out of it. Eventually, the old society had to go, and a new one had to take its place. Which came in the form of Sun Yat-sen and his Xinhai revolution, overthrowing the Qing dynasty in 1911 and ending the mandate of heaven that had begun when Qin Shi Huang united the warring states of China in 221 BC. Following a warlord era, a Japanese invasion, a communist civil war, a state-sponsored famine, a cultural revolution, and the opening up of China to the world, China has learned from its previous mistakes. No longer will China slip into a culture of conservatism, complacency, and laziness. For China is modernizing, investing heavily in telecommunications, railways, artificial intelligence, and electrical projects.

And yet, what has the United States done? Nothing. Like China before, the United States' culture of conservatism and complacency has come back to bite its own tail. Chinese manufacturing once became dead due to cheaper products from the United States. Now, American manufacturing became dead due to cheap products from China. Or as Donald Trump once put it, "It used to be that cars were made in Flint, and you couldn't drink the water in Mexico. Now, cars are made in Mexico, and you can't drink the water in Flint."

But geography alone can't dictate cultures or the rise and fall of nations. The authors Tim Marshall, Robert Kaplan, and Peter Zeihan may center their viewpoint on geography, but it is only a half-response. This, of course, does not disprove their works. I have read a lot of their books and am a big fan of their works and would recommend it to everyone reading this.

Indeed, this book centered more so around James Robinson and *Why Nations Fail,* but it is more than that.

Let us take, for example, the conservative revolution of the 1970s that swept both the United States and the West in general, coupled with the rise of Islamist movements in the Middle East. People like Margaret Thatcher and Ronald Reagan were the top figures of the day, motivated as well by the rise of libertarian thinkers like Milton Freidman and Ayn Rand. Yet today, such figures are no longer seen as mainstream in the west. Britain's labor party has moved from the neoliberal third way policies of Tony Blair to the more socialist policies of Jeremy Corbyn, now Keir Stramer. Yet in the United States, Ayn Rand and Milton Friedman's ideas are still promoted even as the outside world no longer does. This showed itself when, at the annual general secretary speech at the UN, Donald Trump praised the ideas of Ayn Rand, only to be laughed out of the room by the other world leaders.

But why was it that Ayn Rand was flourished in the United States while being rejected elsewhere? Why is it that the New Deal Program was so thoroughly opposed to the point where the 1936 Republican Platform was one of abolishing Social Security? What is different about the United States that would explain this? To answer this question, we must look at history.

The first people to have arrived in what would become the United States were English colonists of the Virginia Colony, establishing Jamestown in 1607. However, as a lot of the activity that ultimately led to the outbreak of the American Revolution began in New England and more specifically, Massachusetts, I will be focusing more on the first people to settle in Massachusetts—the Pilgrims of Mayflower.

It is a common misconception that Thanksgiving commemorates the arrival of the Pilgrims to the shores of America and the establishment of Plymouth Colony. The modern-day holiday of Thanksgiving, celebrated every year on the last Thursday of November, only goes as far back as the Lincoln Administration. Thanksgiving was meant as a day of national unity in the midst of the Civil War, with the notion of it having to do with the Mayflower and Massosoit being a recent invention. Nonetheless, the image has permeated the American psyche to the point where many Native American Activist groups want the holiday banned. Not as a holiday of national unity but as a holiday commemorating the founders of America with their founding ideals. So what, then, were the ideals of the Plymouth colony?

The Pilgrims were religious Puritans, and a central point of their leaving England for the New World was to escape religious and sectarian violence that was wreaking havoc throughout England at this time. I will delve more into religion in the next chapter. Puritans, the most radical devotees of the Calvinist faith, believed not just in the standard hard labor of all the Protestant sects but that you have to endure a great deal of suffering in order to prove your worthiness into heaven, as predetermination was a central part of Calvinist faith. The

Pilgrims were, as a result of their beliefs, in a continuous state of tensions with the crown. Ultimately showing itself when King Charles II, after ousting Oliver Cromwell and his Puritans from power in 1660 and restoring the monarchy, refused to come to the aid of the New England colonists when the Wampanoags, under Chief Metacomet, allied with other Native American tribes to expel the colonists from New England during King Philip's War of 1675–1676.

This central tenet of Puritan ideology, that to achieve salvation in heaven, you must undergo trials and tribulations and not engage in sinful activities, forms the basis for the root cause of why America is a backward nation—the glorification of suffering and hardship. This central theme will be the main basis of the rest of the book. It is also this central thesis that explains why Ayn Rand and Milton Friedman were able to gain such popularity, and why they are still praised by many even as the rest of the world ridicules them. The glorification of suffering and hardship explains a lot as to why America has not been able to fix its social ills. While they may be nice things to have, as you have predetermined your allotted life, such notions should not be considered. While it would be nice to have healthcare provided to you without hesitation, a nice well-paying job without fear of outsourcing, good education, and a nice house, if you were conceived out of the lucky sperm club, your purpose in life is to toil through these things until your reach the zenith. What that zenith is and when you get there, no one really knows.

This attitude of "might makes right," however, has its problems. Indeed, it is no coincidence that countries that promote egalitarian values have the strongest social safety nets. Indeed, a culture of "might makes right" promotes the idea of people falling through the cracks. This is shown through the catastrophic economic fallout of coronavirus. The reason why so many people suffered is because of cultures that not only allows it but glorifies it. Indeed, there is also a historical precedent for this. No civilization embraced the attitude of "might makes right" than the Roman Empire. Indeed, it is also no coincidence that nations with more egalitarian values have less corruption than nations with patriarchal attitudes.

Rome is often viewed by America and the rest of the Western world as the ideal form of government. Yet one simple question is never asked. If the Roman republic was so wonderful, why is it that it collapsed into an empire? Why did the democratic institutions gave way to an oligarchy where the wealthy stopped paying their taxes? And the democratic systems devolved into power, being centered into a hands of a small elite, first civil war between Marius and Sulla, then the triumvirate between Julius Caesar, Pompey, and Marcus Licinnius Crassus; till eventually only Octavius was left standing after defeating Cleopatra and Marc Anthony in the Battle of Actium and dissolved the republic to become the first Roman emperor? Rome should be studied, but it should be studied as a warning. Indeed, I fear that once again the die has been cast as a new Caesar has crossed the Rubicon.

It is through this prism that we are able to find the answer to another question: Why does America have a massive problem with race relations? As I write, protests are erupting over Geroge Floyd, Breonna Taylor, Jacob Blake, and many others; African Americans who have fallen victim to being in police custody. The answers given by people have been widely different. Some people have said individual attitudes. But that doesn't explain racial gaps in wealth, standard of living, healthcare quality, quality of education, and more. Others have said it is purely a systemic thing, and that to end racism, we must end the system. This, however, is also flawed, and it doesn't address people who hold white supremacist views. Some will say it's both. Yet that, too, doesn't address people who, despite not having a racist bone in their body, would not really do anything to change the system. And even these three explanations are missing something.

Something that becomes a lot more evident when you factor in the idea of "predetermination." There are white people out there who are concerned about the overreaches of government and terrified about the prospects of government power yet denounce the Black Lives Matters protests. Why? Because of the notions of predetermination. Just as how the allotted position in life for the white man is to not have healthcare provided for him by the state. It is the allotted role in life for the Black man to have to live in a rough neighborhood and have a few run-ins with cops. In essence, "I have accepted that I will undergo hardships in my life, why can't those negroes do the same?" Indeed, those who claim to not be racist yet still cling on to this set of beliefs may need to question as to whether or not they truly are racist.

Following the American Revolution, America underwent a period of industrialization and Westward expansion. As a result of the Civil War, the United States suffered a massive labor shortage. Fortunately for the United States, the Irish Potato Famine, the Revolutions of 1848, and the unification of Germany and Italy caused severe socio-political disruption in Europe that caused floods of people to immigrate from Europe to the United States. At the same time, Chinese were brought in to work on the railroads. All of this brought about a new fundamental sentiment in America. The French Revolution and the Latin American Wars of Independence were inspired by the American Revolution. Later on, Ho Chi Minh himself would cite the Declaration of Independence. All of these people were immigrating to the United States in droves, citing America as a "land of opportunity." Meanwhile, no one was emigrating from the United States. What was it about the United States that made so many people want to come here? Is there something inherently unique about the United States? The result of divine intervention? Eventually, this speculation was answered in the form of Frederick Jackson Turner in his 1893 book, *The Significance of the Frontier in American History*, which brought about the idea of the Frontier Thesis. That it was the frontier that established American democracy, and the pioneers of the frontier gave rise to the American folk hero, people like Ethan Allen, Davy Crockett, and Daniel Boone.

Two main consequences occurred as a result of Frederick Jackson Turner and his frontier thesis. First, it solidified amongst Americans the notion that, yes, there is something inherently special about the United States in an idea that would forever be known as "American exceptionalism." The reason why this was able to flourish so rapidly was largely simple. Trade and commerce foster an exchange of ideas, and thus, a change of social attitudes. European nations constantly engaged in trade and commerce amongst themselves. So ideas, such as the reformation, the enlightenment, and the democracy were able to spread as they complemented and critiqued each other and themselves. But America has no such trade. It had no need to look outward. Everyone was flocking to America.

Now, this notion was flawed on a simple premise—it wasn't true. Mainly being that America was not the only nation experiencing floods of immigrants during this time. All of the New World nations were experiencing waves of immigrants. Mexico had a large influx of German immigrants. Argentina had a large wave of Italians. Peru had a large wave of immigrants from Japan.

But the second consequence had a much bigger effect. It instilled in the American mindset the idea of "great man history." That what made America possible was only the result of a few great men. Some of these are founders, like Washington and Jefferson. Others are presidents like Lincoln and Grant, but no one was more affected than people of big business. People like Cornelius Vanderbilt, Jay Gould, Andrew Carnegie, John D. Rockefeller, Henry Ford, and many others. As a result, the big businessman became people to look up to. It was men like Morgan and Vanderbilt that made America possible. Everyone wanted to be like Rockefeller.

In it came the idea of "you built that." That one should take pride in one's own achievements. Now, there is nothing inherently wrong with that belief but adding the notion that one has to endure hardship to endure a zenith, the idea of "you built that" transformed into this notion. That unless you endured as much hardship, you worked just as hard, you had no right to complain about anything. Did you build the railroad? No? Then, you have no right to complain that the trains aren't running on time. Did you build the success that is Amazon? No? Then, you have no right to complain about how Jeff Bezos treats his workers.

There were problems with this belief too. Firstly, it wasn't solely the free market that built America. The transcontinental railroad wasn't the result of the free market, thinking it was a good idea, but a specific government policy enacted under the Lincoln Administration. But the second result was much larger. It promoted a false image on who people thought these people were, rather than who they really were. Many of these people were not pioneers but were robber barons who exploited everyone beneath them for their own benefit. It would take the publishing of pieces of literature such as Upton Sinclair's *The Jungle* and other muckrakers like Ida Tarbell and Jacob Riis for their image to be revealed, to be nothing more than a mirage. Nonetheless, the image persisted and still continues to persist. While there are a few outliers, notably Howard Zinn's *A People's History of the United States,* most history works still centered around this idea of great man history. Such as those by Ron Chernow and David McCullough. (It is noteworthy, however, that Ron Chernow and David McCullough are not the worst offenders. (I still read their books and highly praise their work.)

A side consequence of this became what historians jokingly call the "Holy Trinity of US History," where American history is overwhelmingly centered around three wars—the American Revolution, the American Civil War, and the Second World War. What makes these three wars stand out from all of the other wars America has fought in? Where other wars are engaged in more nuanced, and even a bit of self-doubt and self-reflection in these three wars, it is easy to paint the United States as glorious heroes coming to save the day. Of which, Hollywood is a major factor in the spreading of this idea. In some films, it is more seen than in others, notably *Independence Day, Inglorious Bastards,* and *The Patriot.* But very few movies have it the other way around, where the US is the bad guy that needs to be beaten by the glorious (insert whatever here).

Take, for example, the Vietnam war film classic *The Deer Hunter.* How much of the film centers around US war atrocities, such as the Mai Lai Massacre or the dropping of agent orange? Instead, we get a feel-good story where soldiers try to recuperate, following being held captive in a Viet Cong POW Camp. This is not to say that *The Deer Hunter* is a bad film. It is a wonderful film, but it is an example of the double standards of Hollywood, due to the desire by American audiences to be in a continuous state of feeling special and good about themselves. American WWII films are "good guys win, bad guys lose, and as always, America prevails" (to paraphrase *V for Vendetta*) films.

German and Russian WWII films, save for Stalinist propaganda films like the 1950 film *The Fall of Berlin*, are WWII films.

This effect of Hollywood war films also has an impact on foreign policy, mainly in the area of counterinsurgency warfare. One has to wonder, why is it that the United States has never won a counterinsurgency war? The answer is relatively simple. Hollywood war films, with good guys, America, defeats bad guys with superior firepower and divine intervention gives the American people the wrong idea of what war is and what war isn't. As John Ngl says in his book, *Learning to Eat Soup with a Knife* (a book you have to read in order to understand counterinsurgency warfare). "Armies are often accused of learning to fight the previous war." Counterinsurgency warfare is different than conventional warfare between two armies. Counterinsurgency warfare is more political than it is military. To understand insurgency, you have to understand the political situation that led to it, and you have to train militaries as such. When dealing with counterinsurgency warfare, militaries should be learning institutions rather than fighting forces.

The United States began to investigate this, following the Vietnam War, and slowly began to reform its military. Until the Reagan administration put a halt to it. Then, in 1990, Iraq's invasion of Kuwait gave the American people a chance to fight a war the only way they knew how—Second World War style. With the United States being the good guy coming to the rescue to save the victim, Kuwait, from the ruthless tyranny of Saddam Hussein. The overwhelming swiftness and success of the war made the US military completely forget about counterinsurgency warfare, which it was Bush Sr. meant when he said following the end of the Gulf War. "We have kicked Vietnam syndrome once and for all." Ten years later, the September eleventh attacks made Bush Jr., a guy who was clearly drunk of Hollywood perceptions of war, the idea of American exceptionalism, and in the shadow of his father, the man who liberated Kuwait and ended the Cold War without ever firing a shot; launch a series of foolhardy crusades of liberation in Afghanistan and Iraq without thinking through the political realities on the ground.

And as much as people like to talk about continuing presence in the Middle East, both its praisers who say America helped rebuild these nations and its critics who say that America has spent too much time engaged in the process of nation building. The simple truth of the matter is that neither of which is true. America has not rebuilt or engaged in nation building in the slightest. No Marshall Plan was done for Iraq and Afghanistan. Many parts of Afghanistan still look as though they were plucked right out of the stone age. Why? Because Hollywood doesn't do Marshall Plans. It does, to once again paraphrase the film *V for Vendetta*, "Good guys win, bad guys lose, and as always, America prevails." Indeed, it is no coincidence that the foreign policy of Hollywood actor, Ronald Reagan, was once of peace through strength. For that is exactly what Hollywood diplomacy is. The reason why America doesn't change its military tactics for counterinsurgency warfare is because the American public itself doesn't want to. And so long Hollywood continues to be one that spews out "good guy America comes to save the day," it will be unwilling to do so.

A second consequence of Hollywood's foreign policy has woefully misled people of what the military is versus what it isn't. There is a general idea of the military being a public service amongst the American people with no political aspirations of their own. Yet this is not the military at all, as any country that has undergone a military coup will tell you. Indeed, the military is, more often than not, an elite body with its own political aspirations. One can look no further to this than the Chilean coup of September 11, 1973. Preceding the coup, the Chilean military lived in gated communities separated from the rest of the Chilean working class.

Eventually, all of this coalesced after the Second World War. When the United States remained the only undamaged industrial power in the world, and the vast amounts of resources, navigable rivers, and arable lands resulted in massive prosperity at home. Now, this had no impact on the people who lived through the war, for they experienced the hardships of both the war and the great depression. But this would have a huge impact on the people who were born and raised in the aftermath of the Second World War—the baby boomers. Looking around at the vast prosperity of the United States compared with the rest of the world at that time, the baby boomers grew up in the surrounding Protestant culture. That suffering is the greatest form of piety in order to achieve greater salvation, that *this* was the zenith.

That the prosperity of the United States was the final culmination of hard labor and toiling through hardships. That the United States worked the hardest over other countries and not the result of more obvious factors—geographic isolation, wartime economic surplus, a vast abundance of resources, and somewhat sheer luck. This ultimately resulted in cracks that would show itself later, as the baby boomers claimed they toiled through hardships in a time of vast economic prosperity. Notions of needing to work more than one job were nonexistent. The price of college hadn't skyrocketed yet. Student loans were not a thing until the Nixon Administration. While the baby boomers would like to think that it was no different from an era than any other, it was a time of toil and turbulence like others, to fight to maintain a good standard of living. It was, in fact, very different, very unique, and very carefree.

But there was a darker element to this. Growing up in the height of the Cold War, under the threat of the red menace, there was a massive anti-communist public relations campaign that had started first by the Eisenhower administration, that ultimately continued until the dissolution of the Soviet Union. This ultimately included, most notably, McCarthy's committee on un-American activities and the persecution of homosexuals. Two acts that eroded American democratic institutions under the guise of ridding the country from suspected communist infiltrators. Add to this was made mandatory the pledge of allegiance in public schools, as well as adding the phrase "under God" to the pledge. A vehement nationalist sentiment was drilled in that instilled the idea that you only had to be one way to be an American. This resulted in the "love it or leave it" mentality. With this mentality now mainstream, particularly in the minds of the baby boomers, any hopes for social change were dashed. For the "love it or leave it" mentality is a fundamentally conservative mentality. Don't like how we do things here? Then leave.

This, coupled with the notions of American exceptionalism, became formed into an idea of American uniqueness. That America must not be like everyone else, for America is not like the other countries, and America is better. Ultimately, the root of this was built out of Cold War rhetoric. That if the communists reject religion, then Americans must be a people who routinely go to church. If the communists embrace collectively, then Americans must be individualistic and show hard work. Cracks would eventually form and show themselves later. More on that later in the book.

One example of this that comes to my mind is during the 2016 presidential elections. In a rather notorious debate where Marco Rubio kept repeating the same talking point over and over again during a spat with Chris Christie of "Let's dispel with this fiction that Barack Obama doesn't know what he's doing, he knows exactly what he's doing." What was it that Barack knows what he was doing that Marco Rubio thought everyone thought he didn't know what he was doing? "He is trying to change this country; he is trying to make America more like the rest of the world; we don't want to be like the rest of the world, we want to be the United States of America." Such rhetoric from Marco Rubio is a consequence of the Cold War mentality that was instilled in the minds of baby boomers at a young age through a massive public relations campaign. If the rest of the world is savage, then America must be civil. And likewise, if the rest of the world is civil, then America, by default, must be savage. It is not just this mentality, but this mentality constitutes a large part of questions. Like why America is the only industrialized nation to not guarantee healthcare or guarantee paid maternity leave. "This is America. We don't do that here. You don't like it? Go to a country that does!"

This maintenance of doing things "the American Way," even if it is not necessarily the right way, has shown itself in other ways. Take, for example, prisons. It is a well-known fact that the United States has the highest rate of recidivism in the developed world. This is, in large part, due to its prison model. America's prison model of "lock them up and throw away the key" is not really followed in the rest of the developed world. Add to that that many other countries have largely gotten rid of the barbaric practice of solitary confinement. And in many other countries, once they return to society, they rarely, if ever, return to prison. Now, a wise person would see that the American model isn't working and that the United States should adopt a different prison model. But that wouldn't be the way that Americans do things so such discussions are off the table.

But now, I will utilize this question to you. If you are growing up in the United States, hearing over and over since before anything else, patriotic rambles about how great America is; then seeing people immigrate to America instead of Americans immigrating elsewhere, and that America is a prosperous country while other countries are still rebuilding, thereby proving the patriotic ramble right; what mentality would be instilled into you?

I know what would be instilled into me.

That Americans are the master race.

Let us take a look at Trump's decision, for example, to make patriotic education mandatory throughout schools. The reason why Trump believes in this fascist concept is because the baby boomer generation was brought up on this fascist concept.

But ultimately, the good times of the 1950s and 1960s, that the baby boomers were accustomed to, didn't last, for it was built on faulty notions. The war resulted in a vast overabundance of resources; in essence, the United States produced more war-related resources than the war required. This was shown most in the large excess of steel and oil. While much of it was sent to other countries as the war destroyed their ability to produce on their own, a lot of it was spent on fueling the new postwar consumer boom. This is shown in architecture. Or to be more precise, why a lot of postwar architecture is made of steel, replacing the earlier art deco style of the 1930s. And yet, while Americans enjoyed their life of luxury, the rest of the world was slowly rebuilding. And because they had a clean slate, they were able to upgrade and modernize their industries.

Yet America had no need to modernize. The model seemed to be working just fine, and if it ain't broke, don't fix it. Yet the modernization made other countries' industries more efficient than the United States. A few of these include minimills, which recycled old steel rather than having to continue extracting for new sources of iron.

As well as just-in-time manufacturing, developed by the Japanese. It transformed manufacturing so that the number of ready-made products that were made were consistent with the demand, instead of the traditional assembly line model which produces a standard amount of products and hopes that the demand is there. Both significantly were more efficient and lowered manufacturing costs. Meaning, that it was cheaper to make products overseas, and with that, American manufacturing collapsed. A few people tried to raise alarm that the structure that the good times of the 1950s and 1960s would collapse in on itself, but they were ignored. America continued to enjoy the fruits of its wartime labor.

This was added by another dilemma. The pinnacles of industry relied heavily on iron and oil. And for a while, it was believed that the United States had the largest amounts of both. Then, it was discovered that the largest amounts of iron were found within the tiny European nation of Luxembourg. On top of that, the largest of large oil deposits in the Middle East and off the coast of Venezuela, previously unable to be extracted by technological barriers, were made accessible due to new innovations in desert and offshore drilling. With that, dependence on American industry waned. Bethlehem steel, once a staple of the might of American industry, became drowned out by newer, more-efficient steel companies from Luxembourg. It collapsed into bankruptcy and became bought by a Luxembourg steel company, which it remains to this day.

Add to that a third dilemma that resulted in further economic stagnation. The young generation that had returned from fighting abroad had wanted to settle down and raise a family. This resulted in a demand for new housing, which the postwar boom could afford. And so, new large scale housing plots began to spring up in rural countryside, notably on Long Island, and was mass-produced. With many houses looking exactly the same to make them quickly available, cheap to make, and cheap to afford.

Now, the development of large housing units after a war is not unique to the United States. Yet there was something unique to this housing boom that previous housing booms did not have—the car. Previous housing boom still followed the traditional walkable grid pattern, with a downtown that boasted a center of commerce that proved to be the center of the town's economy. But with the car, new housing plots began to revolve around the car. The post-WWII suburban sprawl didn't have a downtown, only a regional shopping mall. The streets were hardly walkable. But no one seemed to mind at first. The car seemed to be a symbol of American individualism. More on that in later chapters. Everyone wanted to drive in their new car, even if it meant things were farther out than they needed to be, more time then driving in their new car. This was followed by the construction of highways that allowed more people to drive their car.

Yet there were problems with the suburban sprawl. This suburban sprawl defied traditional human growth, that human beings evolved to live in clusters in large urban areas. Similar to the large clusters you find in every other social species. This one, one the other hand, was designed to evenly distribute the population with all the amenities of an urban environment. Yet in desiring all the amenities of the urban world with the peace and tranquility of the rural one, neither was achieved. On top of that, as these new suburban developments had no town center, as they were meant as commuter towns while you worked in the city, the towns had to spend more on infrastructure costs than the town generated in revenue, causing many towns to bankrupt. Add to that, the growth of the suburbs resulted in the decline of the cities as the tax base needed to maintain the costs of upkeep for the city was drained out from them.

A lot of people ask the question: What caused the decline of Detroit? While a lot of people have given a lot of different answers, to me, the answer is relatively simple. Following the Second World War, everyone moved out to the suburbs, and thus, the city's tax base collapsed from within.

There was also another darker element to the suburbs. They were not for everyone, just for whites, as was a good chunk of housing development projects throughout American history. This severely increased the racial disparity in America, even as the civil rights movement ended others. Tensions would eventually boil over in the "Ghetto Riots" of the 1960s and 1970s. The largest of these would be the "Long Hot Summer" of 1967, but the situation did not improve. In many respects, it got worse.

Let's take the recent internet phenomena of the "Karen." What should strike about them to anyone is that most Karens that appear on viral videos are not rural rednecks but from well-off suburban neighborhoods. The reason for the suburbs producing such an affluent number of Karens is relatively simple. The design of the suburbs inevitably resulted in this mentality from the people who grew up in them. This is not to say that living in an all-white neighborhood inherently makes one a racist, but living in a neighborhood that was designed to be only for whites would.

The suburbs also created another side effect. In a city, everything is constantly changing. In the suburbs, all the houses look the same, so there is no class distinction. All the people look the same since no Blacks were allowed in the suburbs. And as political activities were banned in shopping malls, a sort of hypnotic twilight zone repetition of "everything is fine, everything is fine, everything is fine, and etc." mentality set in. One that would encourage and enforce conformity among everyone who lived there.

Further, a lot of highways, rather than going around the cities in ring roads as in Europe, they would plow right through the cities. Gutting entire neighborhoods, further declining the cities. In particular minority neighborhoods, more often than not being no coincidence. This practice would only stop when more affluent urban neighborhoods would be up for the chopping block, in particular SoHo, but by then, the damage had been done.

All of these different factors, American manufacturing becoming less efficient. The United States having to compete with other nations. The rise of foreign sources of oil and natural resources, the decline of cities, and increasing racial disparity culminating in massive social unrest were on the seat of the Oval Office when Richard Nixon became president in 1969. Nixon attempt to counteract this and starve of an inevitable collapse of the American society, mainly by taking the dollar off of the Gold Standard and terminating the Bretton Woods system. This was done slowly at first. But when other countries saw what was going on and began to take back their gold,

Nixon had no choice but to pull the plug, doing so in an Oval Office speech delivered on Sunday, August 15, 1971. In addition, to cope with increasing energy demands caused by the postwar consumerism boom, Nixon ended the quota system that had been in place since the Eisenhower administration that was designed to make sure that America never became dependent on foreign sources of energy.

Yet they never worked to the extent that they had hoped. The war in Vietnam and Watergate investigations derailed any attempts on the part of the Nixon administration to transition the economy and prepare for the inevitable end to the postwar economic slow-down. Add to that, the United States' support for Israel during the Yom Kippur War led to the Arab States boycotting oil to the United States and Europe. Severely damaging the economies of these regions, followed by the inevitable collapse of the steel industry soon after. The successive presidents of Ford and Carter proved too weak and unable to steer the ship around.

While all this happened, the baby boomers, now grown up, began to look around. The world of the late 1970s was very different from the one they grew up in. The era of prosperity was clearly over. Now, it was time to adapt. To compete once again on the world stage with China, Japan, Europe, South Korea, and other nations.

All of this put together, the situation reached its climax on the night of July 15, 1979, when United States president, Jimmy Carter, delivered an Oval Office address, one of the most well-known presidential speeches in history. It was known as the "Malaise" speech. It seeks to resolve a fundamental question. Why in the 1970s the United States endured a severe recession, energy crisis, and rapid inflation? For Jimmy Carter, the answer was abundantly clear. The problems facing the United States were the direct result of the postwar consumer boom of the 1950s and 1960s. And that in order to tackle these problems, the United States needed to endure a long and painful large-scale mobilization on a scale not seen since WWII, with gasoline rations, mandatory carpooling, and other measures to tackle the challenges of the 1970s. Also measures that would be needed to tackle climate change, only on a much larger scale.

For the older generation, this was not a big deal. Having been through both the Great Depression and WWII, they were used to having to live with less that Jimmy Carter was instructing the American people to do. But for the younger generation, the baby boomers, they had never experienced having to live with less. They had known no world other than that of mass consumerism. They had no idea how to compete with the rest of the world. All they were ever taught in school was that America is the greatest country in the world. They rejected Jimmy Carter's calls to learn to live with less, and due to the Watergate scandal, they rejected Jimmy Carter's call to once again trust the institutions of government.

This showed itself in the 1980 election, when a Hollywood actor turned governor of California. Ronald Reagan ran for President on an anti-government platform and promised to return to the carefree prosperity of the 1950s and 1960s. More than that, Ronald Reagan, being a man of Hollywood, ran on a platform of Hollywood foreign policy. The foreign policy of "good guy America comes to save the day" after the 1970s saw a decline in patriotism from the defeat in Vietnam, as well as the civil rights movement and a resurgence of Native American activism culminating in the Wounded Knee stand-off of 1973.

But to this flag-draped, anti-government patriotism was a darker meaning. During the entire time, Reagan constant railed against the "welfare queens" and "lazy bums," blaming them for the economic crisis. Not unlike the Nazi rhetoric that was used as an excuse of what went wrong for Germany. While this horrified older voters who knew first hand of the atrocities committed by the atrocities, for the baby boomers, this was irrelevant. As the big threat was not fascism but communism. After all, if Nazi Germany was so bad, then why did we hire many of their top officials in NASA? Wouldn't it have been better if the United States and Nazi Germany formed an alliance to put an end once and for all to the Soviet threat? Why was it that the Nazi Party was backed by big businesses in the hopes that they would be the one to defeat the rising communist movement? Why was it that the Nazis started off as street gangs looking for communists to beat up on the street? To the baby boomers, having grown up in a continuous time of anti-communist hysteria—the Nazis. And thus, Nazi ideology and Nazi rhetoric were the lesser of two evils and only a minor nuisance.

And like Germany in 1933 before hand, the baby boomers, rejecting Carter's words of Malaise, looked to someone to provide simple straight answers about how the establishment is out to get them. Reagan provided one. It wasn't because the postwar consumerism of the baby boomers had caused a mass depletion of their energy reserves and the failure to modernize industry resulted in a loss of efficiency. No, it was because the government taxed and spent too much! (Gee, why didn't anyone think of that before?) Such simple rhetoric fit more to a generation because they did not know of economic hardship like the Great Depression their parents knew. They couldn't comprehend a life without the consumerism that defined the postwar era.

In addition, the race gap that defined the suburban sprawl of the postwar era also showed in the response to Reagan rallying against the "rotten elements" that caused the cities to decline. To the baby boomers, embellished in a culture of personal responsibility and unaware of why their mostly white suburbs were so much better than the mostly Black cities. Maybe it was the fault of the Blacks, maybe they were unable to maintain cities. Through it, more and more, the counterculture revolution that defined the baby boomers in 1968 had been eroded. And the baby boomers reverted back to the conservatism of before, and in one eighty, Ronald Reagan was elected in a landslide. There was no doubt about it now. The baby boomers had spoken, and Ronald Regan was their president.

This legacy has ramifications that exist today. When Richard Nixon was caught ordering a break-in to his political rival's headquarters, he ultimately received public scrutiny and was forced to resign in disgrace. Whereas, when Ronald Reagan was caught committing high treason by subverting Congress in order to fund right wing rebels in Nicaragua using drug money, not only was he not impeached. But he still remains a highly respected figure, rather than receiving the same public scrutiny that Nixon faced. This deification of Ronald Reagan and ignoring of the crimes he committed can be traced to the baby boomers.

A couple of years after Ronald Reagan completed his time as president, the Soviet Union collapsed, ending the Cold War, and ushering in America's "decade of innocence" that defined the administration of President Bill Clinton. With this, came the post-Cold War generation, known as Generation Y or the millennials. Free from the anti-communist state rhetoric that had defined the childhood of the baby boomers, the one of the millennials was defined by globalization and internationalism, as well as the internet putting a vast amount of knowledge at their fingertips. And with it, came a new perspective on society. With the ability to see beyond the confines of their own borders for the first time, millennials saw other countries in a way that previous generations never could. And with the dissolution of borders came the dissolution of nationalist tendencies. While previous generations were brought up on the idea of "American exceptionalism," millennials were brought up on the idea that there is nothing inherently special about America. America was not the only democracy in the world.

Also with the internet, came new realities and experiences. With information being so limited, it was a lot easier to be controlled. But it was no longer case with internet. With the abundance of knowledge, there came new ways of thinking. Because of that, old concepts about what socialism was changed as they were no longer subject to vast anti-communist hysteria. While other people think about socialism, they may think about Stalin's Gulags or Mao's famine. When I think of socialism, I think of a spectrum of various ideologies. While others, when they think of Bernie Sander's vision of Democratic Socialism, think of North Korea. When I hear Bernie Sanders's vision of Democratic Socialism, I think of David Ben-Gurion and the Israeli kibbutz model which, if you read his own autobiography, you will find was a much bigger impact on his worldview than anything Karl Marx ever said.

But the largest impact of the dismantling of nationalism caused by a more globalized world was that, as the old lenses of American exceptionalism became thrown off, millennials looked at America in a more critical light. All the inequalities that America had begun to come through, and more and more Americans began to question why it is that their country is the way it is. If America is so great, why don't we have a robust rail network? If America is so great, why didn't we establish a national health service after the Second World War like Britain did?

Also added to this was another change—the evolution of television. Previous generations had grown up on TV shows like *The Waltons, Leave It to Beaver, Father Knows Best, The Andy Griffith Show,* and others. All of these centered around a common theme—instilling the values of what the ideal American family ought to be with these families living in utopian small-town America. While the families were not real, they were idealistic. They instilled into the minds of those watching that this is what American family life ought to be. But later generations grew up on different types of TV shows. For earlier millennials, it was *The Simpsons.* For later millennials and going into Gen Z, *SpongeBob.* Both of these shows were immensely counter-culture, *The Simpsons* more so. And dealt with major societal issues and openly mocked American values, as George H.W. Bush's comment "Make American families a lot more like *The Waltons* and a lot less like *The Simpsons*" testified to. While *The Simpsons* is seen as a stable of American culture today, one must not forget how controversial it was in the 1990s, due to the fact that it did the one thing Americans didn't want—it rocked the boat.

Ultimately, this caused a severe rift between the younger millennials and older baby boomers. And it reflected in their politics, as younger people become more and more disgusted with the political system and wanted something new. And so, because of this, the contents of this book here will largely be driven at an audience that doesn't quite understand the calls for a new perspective and who can't understand why someone like Alexandria Ocasio Cortez exists. With that in mind, I will begin this with the first segment of the book—the church.

CHAPTER 2

On the Nature of the Church

Mother Teresa was not a friend of the poor. She was a friend of poverty. She said that suffering was a gift from God. She spent her life opposing the only known cure for poverty, which is the empowerment of women and the emancipation of them from a livestock version of compulsory reproduction. Many more people are poor and sick because of the life of Mother Teresa. Even more will be poor and sick if her example is followed. She was a fanatic, a fundamentalist, and a fraud, and a church that officially protects those who violate the innocent has given us another clear sign of where it truly stands on moral and ethical questions.

—Christopher Hitchens

One thing that has struck me throughout my life, as I have spent a considerable amount of time in inner cities, is the amount of new churches that you will find throughout the inner cities even as everything else crumbles around them. It's amazing how there is no money for schools, homes, maintaining the sidewalks, and parks, yet there is always enough money for a brand-new church.

The dominant religion of America is Christianity. More specifically, various dominions of the Protestant sect of Christianity, with its roots going back to the Pilgrims as I mentioned earlier. Christianity is a religion that claims to be a religion of peace, and yet, Christianity has never once been in tolerance with those outside of their domain. Everyone had to learn of the "peaceful" message of Jesus Christ. And if they had no intention to convert on their own, then war it is. From the persecution of Jews to the Crusades, to the mass conversion and extermination of indigenous peoples, to calls to make the west guide more in line with Christian ideals. One has to ask oneself, why, in the face of all this damning historical evidence, do we still believe that Jesus was a man of peace and love? It is time for the Christian world to take the mirage of who they think Jesus was, to make themselves feel better about the numerous atrocities they committed in his name and start to see him for who he really was. After all, Buddha also preached tolerance and love, and yet, apart from the Rohingya genocide, I can't think of any religious wars that started in the name of Buddha.

And the fact that rundown inner cities have so many churches brings about another fundamental aspect of religion. Why is it that as societies got richer, they got less religious? Simple. Religion, like alcohol, acts like a cage that perpetually traps you into a state of isolation. The worst part being that you do not know how much in a state of desolation you are. For religion, ultimately, teaches you that things will eventually get better, if not in this life, then in the next. Let's take the Black community as an example. Religion, more specifically Southern Baptism, has been an integral part of the Black community since the days of slavery. Yet if the Black community wants to truly be free, they must break free not only from the forces of state oppression but from the forces of religion. After all, those in the Black community who claim that it was their faith in Jesus that got them out of slavery would do well to remember Ephesians 6:5.

Now, if you haven't gotten the gist of it by now, yes, I am that atheist asshole. Yet I will not be spending time debunking various religions. Rather, I will instead be analyzing greater societal and sociological trends about what it means to be religious.

It is no secret that America has a long history of being a religious country. This effect has had a lasting legacy on the psyche of the country, even those who don't believe in religion may still find themselves religious.

This, of course, begs the question: What does it mean to be religious? To be religious about something is to believe in the existence of some form of higher power, while religion is an organized institution revolved around said higher power. You can make a religion out of anything (as anyone who has spent any time in a modern social justice activist circle will tell you), and you don't have to go to church to be religious.

Let's take the issue of gun violence for an example. It is not that the NRA secretly loves the fact that so many people are dying by gun violence, but rather, the deaths of these people are a necessary price to pay for the greater good of the Second Amendment. Much like how Jesus died for the sins of humanity, these people died for the Second Amendment.

So if not Christianity or any of the other recognized religions, what is there to be religious about?

Capitalism.

In the previous chapter, I mentioned the Jamestown Colony only briefly. I will go into it further.

The Jamestown Colony is often told in a romantic way, with the brave explorer Sir John Smith arriving in an unknown place. Only to be greeted by hostile Indians that would have killed them until Pocahontas rushed in to save them, and they all lived happily ever after. But that is not the case at all. The Jamestown Colony was established by the Royal Virginia Company with the sole purpose of extracting the resources of the area for profit, regardless of what the local Powhatan thought. Rather than having lived in peace, the two engaged in to wars with each other, with numerous instances of Jamestown colonists shooting at Powhatan children for fun as they tried to swim across one of the various rivers of the Chesapeake Bay area for safety.

The first colony was devoted entirely to business. The second colony was devoted entirely to religious fundamentalism. And modern America is their offspring. A religious fundamentalist devotion to capitalism. A capitalist version of Sharia law. In essence, free market totalitarianism.

In hearing about the constant praising of the free market by Americans, my mind comes to North Korea. For North Korea is not just the worshiping of Kim Il Sung, Kim Jong Il, and Kim Jong Un (and maybe Kim Yo Jung, who knows) but praising of the ideals of Juche. For the Arirang Mass Games, the largest mass games in the world, the games are in celebration, not of the leaders but of Jucheism.

Now, some will respond if this is a totalitarian state? Where are the secret police? It is true, there are no secret police that arrest those that publish statements critical of the free market. That is because there is no need to. For the mob mentality of the American people substitutes for secret police. I am sure that many Americans, while rejecting the fact all North Korean music must glorify the regime, would not object to the fact the all music the Americans are allowed to listen to must glorify the free market. Or to the idea of holding mass games in celebration of the free market. For in America, the free market, like God, is all-knowing and all good, ignoring of course the atrocities committed in its name. Such as the cruelty of the East India Company or the slave labor in the Belgian Congo that was instrumental to the industrial revolution of the late nineteenth and early twentieth centuries. This is evident in the religious rhetoric that Americans use about the free market—"God is good, the free market is good. God works in mysterious ways. The free market works in mysterious ways. Put for faith in God, put your faith in the free market." To paraphrase George Carlin, "Teach them that the invisible hand of the free market will solve all their problems, and they believe you. Teach them that the paint is wet, and they have to touch it to be sure."

Like Protestantism, a central tenant about being religious about the free market is one. Not just about personal responsibility but personal repentance. For in the Puritan belief, one is born hated by God and must spend their entire life repenting for their sins in the hopes that God will eventually forgive them and grant them into heaven. Likewise, the same is true with free market worshippers. There are many people who are in the lower middle class who struggle with high bills, medical and student loan debt. And yet, when someone comes along to restructure the system by establishing a national health service where the costs are paid like all other public services with a system that means that people with more money pay more in taxes, lowering the burden on middle and working class Americans. They immediately reject such a proposal, saying that it is worse than the experience they have now.

But why? Because then their suffering would have been in vain. And a central tenet of Puritan belief is that one's suffering must not be in vain. And so, much like the monks of medieval Europe who whipped themselves on the back to prove themselves worthy of God's redemption and admittance into the heavenly kingdom, Americans will prefer to undergo the stress of having the burden be born completely upon oneself in order to prove themselves worthy. Worthy of what? I don't know, with the usual platitudes of "I can do this" or "It's all my doing" or "I just need to work harder." In order for Americans to break free of their woes, they must come to learn that there is more to their troubles than just themselves. That it is okay to say, "I don't need to bear this." For true secularism does not mean the absence of Christianity, but the absence of a notion of some higher institution that you can rely on for your woes.

The idea of the free market and private entrepreneurs coming to save the day that has been so enveloped into American education is, however, based on a series of lies. The big one is that America, by the start of the twentieth century, had built this industrial might without the support of the government. This, however, is not true. By the time America had its first underground subway network, they had already been a thing in many European cities for decades. The first one being in London in 1863. During WWII, Eisenhower was impressed with the German highway network and wanted to replicate that here. Indeed, American history is a history of falling massively behind other countries, then rapidly catching up, then acting like they were ahead of everyone else the whole time.

Nor is true that the free market is the best remedy for everything. One immediately comes to mind—the Italian Wars, where the armies used mainly mercenaries from Switzerland to fight. One of those armies was led by Ludovico Sforza, who was betrayed by his own mercenaries after the French promised him higher pay. Something a young Nicolo Machiavelli witnessed and was instrumental in forming his staunch opposition to private armies.

This, of course, brings Americans into conflict with the main opposition to the private sector—government. Which brings me to my next chapter, the role of government.

CHAPTER 3

On the Role of the Government

If you have selfish, ignorant citizens, you are gonna get selfish, ignorant leaders.

—George Carlin

Acommon misconception that Americans are taught is that power inherently corrupts. It does not, rather it inherently exposes the corrupted. For in a democracy, elected leaders are a representation of the people they elect.

Likewise, if you want to understand the failures of government, you must understand the failure of the society that elects government. It is a common mentality that you see going around the United States that "it isn't the role of government to do this." And ultimately, this manifests itself in the form of government inaction. In a sense, you can't say that it isn't the government's role to do anything and then complain that the government isn't doing anything.

Americans will look at the failure of government and of politicians and say, "It's their fault. It's lobbyists. It's *everyone else* but them. It's *everyone* else's rhetoric but their own. It's *everyone* else's selfishness but their own".

For if honest Americans were placed with an honest American as President, what would they want him to do? Go before the American people in an Oval Office speech and say, "It's not my job to work to make your lives better, all of you can fuck off?"

Let us take, as an example to compare, the prostitution industry. Currently, it is, for the most part, illegal in the United States, and so it thrives only in the black market. The prostitution industry is also riddled with STDs. But if you will recall, I said for the most part. For just outside Las Vegas, it is legal. And there, you will find no STDs. As is the case in the Netherlands or any other part of the world where it is legal. That is because since it is out of the black market, people can work to address its flaws. Likewise, the same is true for the government. The reason the government has problems is because the people don't want to deal with the government and confine it to the black market, where, once there, no one will care what happens to it. Government reform requires a real fundamental acceptance of the place of government in public society, not just say it but work to privatize it as much as possible.

They say that the definition of insanity is to do the same thing over and over and expect different results. Americans like to say that more than anyone, yet they do not understand the irony of that statement. For, if that is the true definition of insanity, Americans are the most insane people on the planet. First, the Americans waged a war on liquor. It didn't work, and there ended up being more liquor. Then, the Americans waged a war on drugs. It didn't work, and there ended up being more drugs. Then, the American people, thinking in sheer stupidity that the third time's the charm, decided to wage a war on the government. And like before, it didn't work, and there ended up being more government than ever before. Indeed, presidents that have waged war on the government have had more government than ever before, as one immediately thinks of George Bush Jr. establishing the Department of Homeland Security. And presidents who waged war on the deficit ended up having a bigger deficit than before. To not have a big government, one must end the war on government.

This, of course, begs the question, what is the role of government? The answer is simple. The role of government is the protection of private property and to serve as a representative to those who do not have the optical power on their own. The role of government is, to put it bluntly, not hope for the best-case scenario and prepare for the worst-case scenario.

Americans, however, despite claiming to be realists, believe in the notion of a nonaggression principle and hope for the best-case scenario. Particularly in the fundamentalist attitudes of the free market, where if only the American people would just tap their heels together three times and say, "There is no place like home, there is no place like home!" Then, the free market will solve anything.

For, like the Pilgrims before, Americans have developed a cultist attitude, with all the heaven and hell that comes with it. Yet they will claim that having cultish attitudes will not come back to haunt them. In which case, all Americans should go and look up "Jonestown, Guyana" and see what happens when you put blind faith in an institution. Whether it is a cult around one man such as Jim Jones or a cult around a vague abstract such as the free market, a cult is still a cult. A cultist is still a cultist. Americans have drunk the Kool-Aid of free market fanaticism and will follow it even if it leads them down a cliff, in a very "Hitler Youth" fashion.

For if the free market cultists are to respond with "I don't believe the free market can solve everything!" I simply answer, "Name one thing that you believe the private sector can do better than the public sector." If you claim to not be a free market cultist, yet when push comes to shove, still pushes for more free market and more private sector, can one really honestly claim they are not a cultist?

This, of course, means that we must break down what the free market is and what it isn't. Note that I make a distinction between capitalism and the free market. They are interconnected, yet they are not the same thing. The free market is built around for-profit notions. There is absolutely no way that anything in the free market and in the private sector cannot be for profit. This, of course, begs the question, "Do you really want to put faith in an institution that is solely around profit?" Would you want to put things like roads, schools, and your health into an institution that is built solely around profit? Or would you want to suffer the same risk that was undertaken by Ludovico Sforza, having private armies fighting only for-profit work for him until someone was willing to pay them more? And Niccolo Machiavelli bucked the trend by saying the notion of private armies and privatization of wars should be abolished, a notion that would not become mainstream in European societies until Napoleon?

And because of the fact that the free market is a for-profit institution predicated on wealth, it only serves those who can afford it. Which once again, begs the question: do you really want to reduce certain institutions to only those who can afford it? Things like justice and defense, can you imagine a notion of a system where it is only people that can afford defense get it?

Another thing Americans must come to term with the free market, in terms of what it is and what it isn't, is the fundamental truth about power. Americans claim that they are skeptical of power, yet they do not understand what it is. The basic truth about power is this: nature abhors a vacuum. Sooner or later, the vacuum will be filled. Those who champion free market competition without government intervention don't understand that the free market competition will eventually give way to monopolization and the consolidation of power, as nature abhors a vacuum. Therefore, it is impossible to just "leave the free market to its whims," and it is impossible to privatize industries that are monopolistic by their very nature.

For example, one goes by train from point A to point B. There is only one train line. Hell, one track that goes between these places. How are you going to privatize an industry that will never have any free market competition whatsoever? One also goes to the austerity policies implemented by Tony Blair on the National Health Service. A devout neoliberal, he tried to prove that you could privatize the NHS by artificially creating free market competition. Which, in the end, didn't work and only resulted in the biggest decline in quality of the National Health Service since it was established by Clement Attlee in 1948.

The fundamental flaw in American logic is that people are predictable. Ironically, it is the one thing that they use to debunk Marxist arguments—the human factor. Some people are predictable. Humans, by and large, are not. This, however, is not unique to right-wing Americans. It is an American problem as a whole, as recent calls from the left to abolish the police altogether and replace it with a utopian idea that humans will look out for each other without a police force. Once again hoping for a best-case scenario, instead of planning for a worst-case scenario.

Therefore, to figure out what should and should not be privatized, is to put it along a four-question questionnaire:

1. Is it a service/industry that you can trust in the hands of someone whose sole purpose is to make a profit?
2. Is it a service/industry that you can comfortably restrict access to only those who can afford it?
3. Is it a service/industry where it is impossible to not have a monopoly of?
4. Will privatizing the service create more or less efficiency?

It is also, therefore, a question of government accountability versus free market accountability. For, if you have a government not doing its job and failing in its duties when things go one, the people can, at least in theory, hold people in power accountable to petitions and ultimately, elections. It doesn't always happen, but there is the possibility of accountability in a way that cannot occur with the free market. If a private company messes up, who has final accountability? Who holds accountability? Do the people vote out the CEO in free and fair elections?

This also brings up the role democracy plays in the role of government. Americans revolted against the crown in favor of democracy, hoping that the role of government shrinks. What Americans don't seem to realize is that in a democracy, the role of government expands. This is basic common sense. If you have a government that gives power to the people, the people will expect more of their government. If you want to stop people demanding more from the government, stop giving the people the power to take part in government and go back to the days of the divine rights of kings. Kings and queens do not care about the general welfare of their subjects, for they are not obligated to.

It is here that we must bring up another (seemingly apparent) element of government, which is bureaucracy. Which begs a question: what exactly is bureaucracy? Bureaucracy is, to be precise, any institution that decides for others what to do. However, Americans, despite claiming to be experts on bureaucracy, do not know what bureaucracy is. If you have a health insurance company that has a panel that decides what doctor is in network, what hospitals are in network, and what medicines are in network, how is that not bureaucracy? And one must ask why Americans, who seemingly are so against the notion of bureaucracy, would be willing to let this go on? Are Americans so hypnotized by the supposed goodness of the free market that because it's a bureaucracy of the private sector, it must be good, or better, by default?

People, of course, like to instead rally behind the question, "The government is overstepping its boundaries!" I, however, respond with Article 1, Section 8 of the United States Constitution, which clearly defines the powers and responsibilities of the federal government, more specifically the Congress. In it, it clearly states that the Congress shall have the power:

To lay and collect Taxes, Duties, Imposts and Excises, to pay the Debts and provide for the common Defense and general Welfare of the

United States; but all Duties, Imposts and Excises shall be uniform throughout the United States;

So the government actually has the power to establish public schools, hospitals, parks, and services like healthcare.

To borrow on the credit of the United States;

Which means that the government has the power to run up a deficit

To regulate commerce with foreign Nations, and among the several states, and with the Indian Tribes;

So the government has the power to regulate businesses and even break up big businesses

To establish a uniform Rule of Naturalization, and uniform Laws on the subject of Bankruptcies throughout the United States;

So the government has the power to establish an immigration policy.

To coin Money, regulate the Value thereof, and of foreign Coin, and fix the Standard of Weights and Measures;

So the government has the power to print money, control inflation, establish price controls, and establish forms of standardization.

To provide for the Punishment of counterfeiting the Securities and current coin of the United States;

So the government has the power to crack down on counterfeiting and other forms of financial fraud, such as embezzling.

To promote the Progress of Science and useful Arts, by securing for limited Times to Authors and Inventors the exclusive Right to their respective Writings and Discoveries;

So the government has the power to establish copyright laws and establish cultural institutions.

To constitute Tribunals inferior to the Supreme Court;

So the government has the power to establish an independent court system.

To define and punish Piracies and Felonies committed on the high Seas, and Offenses against the Law of Nations;

So the government has the power to regulate maritime activities that takes place within its domain, from piracy to offshore drilling.

To declare War, grant Letters of Marque and Reprisal, and make Rules concerning Captures on Land and Water;

So the government has the power to make laws concerning the rules of warfare.

To raise and support Armies, but no Appropriation of Money to that Use shall be for a longer Term than two Years;

So the government has the power to fund a military.

To provide and maintain a Navy;

So the government has the power to fund a navy.

To make Rules for the Government and Regulation of the land and naval Forces;

So the government has the power to establish laws concerning the distribution of weapons, such as guns.

To provide for calling forth the Militia to execute the Laws of the Union, suppress Insurrections and repel Invasions;

So the government has the power to crack down on militia groups and extremists, such as the Branch Davidians.

To provide for organizing, arming, and disciplining, the Militia, and for governing such Part of them as may be employed in the Service of the United States, reserving to the States respectively, the Appointment of the Officers, and the Authority of training the Militia according to the discipline prescribed by Congress;

So the government has the power to enforce a draft.

To exercise exclusive Legislation in all Cases whatsoever, over such District (not exceeding ten Miles square) as may, by Cession of particular States, and the Acceptance of Congress, become the Seat of the Government of the United States, and to exercise like Authority over all Places purchased by the Consent of the Legislature of the State in which the Same shall be, for the Erection of Forts, Magazines, Arsenals, dock-Yards, and other needful Buildings;

So the government has the power to establish a federal district to serve as the nation's capital and build military bases.

—And

To make all Laws which shall be necessary and proper for carrying into Execution the foregoing Powers, and all other Powers vested by this Constitution in the Government of the United States, or in any Department or Officer thereof.

So the government has the power to enforce its powers through laws.

When one analyzes this, it becomes rather obvious that none of what people like Bernie Sanders and Alexandria Ocasio-Cortez are proposing is unconstitutional or an overreach of government power. And to be more precise, the next section of the United States Constitution, Article 1, Section 9, discusses what the government *can't* do.

The Migration or Importation of such Persons as any of the States now existing shall think proper to admit, shall not be prohibited by the Congress prior to the Year one thousand eight hundred and eight, but a Tax or duty may be imposed on such Importation, not exceeding ten dollars for each Person.

So the slave trade cannot be legal beyond 1808.

The Privilege of the Writ of Habeas Corpus shall not be suspended, unless when in Cases of Rebellion or Invasion the public Safety may require it.

So the government cannot suspend Habeas Corpus except in time of national emergency.

No Bill of attainder or ex post facto Law shall be passed.

So the government can't declare someone guilty without trial or make criminal actions that were legal at the time.

No Capitation, or other direct, Tax shall be laid, unless in Proportion to the Census or Enumeration herein before directed to be taken.

So the government can't tax income (This was later rescinded with the passage of the Sixteenth Amendment).

No Tax or Duty shall be laid on Articles exported from any State.

So the government can't tax goods that go in between the state.

No Preference shall be given by any Regulation of Commerce or Revenue to the Ports of one State over those of another: nor shall Vessels bound to, or from, one State, be obliged to enter, clear, or pay Duties in another.

So the government can't lay tariffs one goods that travel from one US port to another US port.

No Money shall be drawn from the Treasury, but in Consequence of Appropriations made by Law; and a regular Statement and Account of Receipts and Expenditures of all public Money shall be published from time to time.

So the government can't ask for money except for appropriations.

No Title of Nobility shall be granted by the United States: And no Person holding any Office of Profit or Trust under them, shall, without the Consent of the Congress, accept of any present, Emolument, Office, or Title, of any kind whatever, from any King, Prince, or foreign State.

So the government can't give anyone a title of nobility or receive a gift from foreign heads of state to any members of public office. Something that needs to be enforced more often.

As you can see, there is nothing that says that the government can't provide social benefit, such as universal healthcare or public education or regulate big business.

But reexamining the role of government requires another change—the fundamental rot in American society and the main problem laid out in this book.

CHAPTER 4

On the Social Contract

You can always count on the Americans to do the right thing, after they've tried everything else.

—Winston Churchill

There are countries out there whose fortunes and misfortunes are determined by the geography in which they reside. Indonesia is an example. A country spreading over thousands of square miles, composed mostly of islands, and populated by various ethnic groups in conflict—a legacy of the Dutch colonial empire. Therefore, to maintain its territorial integrity, the average Indonesian federal budget is relatively simple. Fifty percent of the budget must be spent on the navy and coast guard to patrol the country's vast territorial waterways. The other 50 percent are to be spent on internal security forces to preserve the country's territorial integrity and fight secessionists, such as those in West New Guinea. No money to be spent on social services or anything that would draw in outside investment. For outside investment would draw in the ability of foreign powers to exploit Indonesia's internal ethnic divisions for their own benefit. Therefore, for the survival of the state, Indonesia must remain poor.

Yet America does not have these problems. The heartland is protected by two mountain ranges on each end. Those mountains anchor two massive oceans that would be very difficult to cross. The heartland also hosts some of the most abundant navigable rivers and arable lands. In addition, there are huge amounts of resources such as oil, coal, and natural gas. Not to mention, the vast potential of renewable energy from geothermal, solar energy in the southwest, and wind in the Great Plains. This makes America secure and self-sustainable in a way no nation on earth is. In fact, it is so self-sustainable that I would argue that it shouldn't matter who is president of the United States, for America can afford to rest easy.

Yet America doesn't have that. It is suffering from massive inequality, social unrest, racial unrest, massive economic insecurities, food insecurities, people unable to get healthcare and housing, and with the coronavirus, causing a massive spike in unemployment. On top of that, every election has proven to be nerve-wracking for so many. Even though the vast amounts of wealth should provide a shield to all this.

This, according to Kaplan or Marshall's view of prosperity, shouldn't make any sense. But it does if we subscribe to the "why nations fail" model of the world. America's problems are not geographical in nature; they are cultural in nature. Confronting America's problems requires confronting America's culture, America's social contract.

Of course, doing so requires doing what I have been doing and have been trying to get you, the reader, to do—look at American culture from the outside looking in. Yet Americans, following generations of geographic and cultural barriers, think they have nothing to learn from the outside world, and instead, the outside world has everything to learn from them. When problems with the American social structure are brought up, the response is very convenient. To present a token immigrant who shares their stories of overcoming obstacles to get here, followed by the cherry on top of "America is the land of opportunity; America is the greatest country of all." And with that, everyone is supposed to shut up. Immigrants come to America to escape state-sponsored persecution of dissidents, only to take part in mob-sponsored persecution of dissidents.

Then, to complete the time-honored American tradition of mass-circle jerking, Americans like to teach themselves that America is the envy of the world. That everyone is jealous of America's success, and everyone wants to mimic them. Who, though, is envious? Jealous of what? America has become the laughingstock of the world, particularly under the Trump administration. Europe is undergoing a policy of becoming a liberal counterweight to the United States, a policy that had begun as a result of the invasion of Iraq in 2003. No country wants to copy America's healthcare system. No country wants to copy America's education system, the obsession with cars, and Black Friday mass-shopping. Europe has very few presidential republics and more parliaments. In fact, the only places that seem to copy the United States system of government are Africa and Latin America, places with third world conditions and governments with a notorious reputation of corruption and dictatorship. Some envy.

Or even the notion that America is leading the world in technological and social innovation. To which I respond, "In what field? The biggest developments in artificial intelligence are being led by the Chinese. The Russians are advancing in hypersonic missile technology. The Japanese are also accelerating in robotics. Online mobile banking was invented in Kenya. What contributions has America made in recent years? What has been taught at American schools and universities? Certainly nothing but standardized tests, and nothing but conformity. Obedience toward God, patriotism, and the free market.

Yet Americans never give credit to any of these countries and civilizations for their contributions to modern humanity. On the contrary, Americans view Europeans as just servants whose whole purpose is to tender the ancient architecture for when Americans come to visit.

America, through years of geographic isolation and mass immigration, has developed a culture that thinks that they have nothing to learn from others and that everyone has something to learn from them. Yet if the average Joe were to meet someone on the street, who thought he had nothing to learn from others, and everyone had something to learn from him, the average Joe would think he was the most arrogant, selfish of men. Being in continuous contact amongst the various European nations forced them to learn from each other, adapt to changing circumstances and new ideas. And because of that, had to confront themselves. Germany has emerged from the rubble of the Second World War to become not just one of the most powerful countries in the world but also a free world counterweight to the United States. Something that would not have been possible if it weren't for Germany confronting its Nazi past.

America, on the other hand, has been unwilling to confront its past and instead calls for "unity." As to what that entails, no one can say, even as the post-George Floyd era is seeing a new wave of clamoring for it. While the extent of Americans failing to confront the past of the United States may not be the same as it is in Turkey or Japan, it is nonetheless evident that America coming apart at the seams is evident of the fact that Americans can't confront the fact that one of their own would like to overthrow its supposed ideals. Why else would right-wing militias continue to roam free, or groups like QAnon able to thrive. After all, a culture that glorifies big business will be one hesitant to confront it even if it commits numerous atrocities, such as big pharmaceutical companies making as many people hooked on dangerous addictive drugs as much as possible in order to make a profit. If you have a culture built upon religious puritanism that refuses to talk about issues, like sexuality, you will continue to face a rampant problem of teen pregnancy or STDs.

Nor can we ignore that, like China before it, America's social conservatism will prove to be a downfall. The world has changed a lot since the Second World War, yet Americans continue their prewar social attitudes as if nothing has changed since then, even if reality comes knocking down their door. This has manifested itself in many cultural stereotypes non-Americans have of Americans. Such as the Swedish saying that when things go bad, they "Americanize" or the saying, "an American travels abroad thinking the whole world is like the United States, whereas a Frenchman travels abroad knowing the rest of the world isn't like France but wishes it were." And of course, the images of Europeans associating Americans at Walmart, with being morbidly obese, driving around on mobile shopping carts with nothing but guns at their disposal. Others may see it as harmless banter, but I see it as part of a deeper problem.

So we have established that America needs to change its social contact. Indeed, we need change its social structure. But what is it that America should change?

One word.

Everything.

The first step would be to understand the roots of the current social contracts, but as I already did it in the first chapter, I will instead be using a comparison template.

Many have asked the question, "Why does Bernie Sanders always bring up Scandinavia?" But that should be followed up with a more interesting question, "Why are the Scandinavians more willing to adopt social democrat policies?" To me, the roots are very simple. The legacy of the egalitarian social structure of Viking society paved the way for the Scandinavians to create an egalitarian series of social policies. One that has made Scandinavia an envy of the world, leading in terms of healthcare, happiness, wages, and etc. This does not mean that Scandinavia is a perfect society. It has problems with alcoholism and high rates of suicides, and I personally prefer the German economic model. But it is nonetheless an example of how the origins of societies and the values preached by those societies at the time could lead to the societies of the day.

For example, in Vikings, women held considerable political power, with the ability to own property and divorce their husbands on their own accord. Today, Scandinavia has often been praised as being the ideal model of a postfeminist society, with Sweden proclaiming a feminist foreign policy. And Finland's first-female prime minister, Sanna Marin, having virtually only women in her government. Although, the fact that the Finnish language has no distinction between he or she of any kind, certainly can be a factor to that as well. Compare that to America, a society founded by religious Puritans, with a deep devotion to religious piety, and women were little more than property.

For America to address its problems, it must get rid of its old social contract and put a new one in its place. Or to paraphrase Russel Means, "For the world to live, the Pilgrims must die." Which, of course, begs the question: What exactly is the social contract?

The social contract is a phrase originally coined by Thomas Hobbes in his book, *Leviathan,* which is the origins of modern western political conservatism. It is an agreement made by the people with their government that a certain amount of their individual liberty would be made in exchange for the security of the greater good of society. Although, it is also an agreement made between one member of the public and another member of the public. Hobbes was of the theory that humans were, by their nature, savages, who, if left to their own nature, would end up killing each other. So it was better to have one person in charge of everyone to keep order. This was in contrast with the founder of modern-day notions of liberalism John Locke, who believed that humans were a mix of different characteristics. And that leaders should only rule and govern with the consent of the people. A third theory eventually developed as well. Developed by Jean-Jaque Rousseau in his books, *Discourse on Inequality* and *The Social Contract,* that believed humans were a social people. That human nature was to do everything in a group, and therefore, the root of all inequality and social injustice was the notion of private property, as it was against human nature. And that humans would be better off overthrowing their monarchs and governing themselves without higher interference, which proved to be the basis for the modern-day notions of socialism.

Although the social contract has only been a notion in the realm of political science since the enlightenment, the truth is the social contract in and of itself has been with humans since the dawn of time. Humans are social animals who like to congregate in groups, and as long as there has been a society, there has been a social contract.

Yet before we delve into the faults with the American social contract and the American concept of a social contract, we, much like how the egalitarian aspect of Viking Society contributed to Scandinavia becoming a beacon for social democracy worldwide, understand how the early American social structure contributed to the modern American social contract. In it, we have the business-orientated Jamestown and the Puritan Plymouth. Therefore, the American social contract is business-orientated and Puritan by its nature.

Therefore, the American social contract was centered around the Puritan belief of the idea of repent—that all humans are born sinners and destined to go to hell. And that only hard work can grant one's acceptance into heaven, only in the place of God. Instead, it is a corporation that we must work in the favor of corporations hard enough to earn their pleasure, and perhaps then, we will earn a better spot in life. In addition, since the Puritan's belief is centered around the notions of individual salvation, Americans have become a culture of rugged individualism. Americans will claim to be a people that promotes the community. But when push comes to shove, they will devolve into a primitive mentality of every man for themselves, constantly fighting with each other until the last man is standing. Did Americans, even once, ever believe in any of the things they claim to espouse?

The American social contract of religious devotion of individualism and one must toil to please an overseer. In this case, big business but even more so. Because all are born sinners, and all must work to repent. Americans have grown a culture that in order for their suffering to not be in vain, their suffering must be implanted onto someone else—the next generation. For Americans do not know how to remove the trauma of living in a cult-environment. And so, to lessen the impact of the trauma, transfers it to someone else, in a continuous cycle of generational trauma, a "I had to endure it, and I don't know how to process it. Therefore, you have to endure it too!" A philosophy that can extend to anything from getting raped to paying off debt. Very often I have heard Americans, mainly older Americans, say some offhanded remarks to the effect of, "Oh, kids these days have it so much easier than we did" in a very negative tone. Implying that they shouldn't have it easier than they did. But isn't that point of societal advancement? Isn't that why, instead of washing your laundry by hand for the entire day, humans invented the washing machine that can do the same thing in an hour? Why do we have machines that can do more productivity in less time? For a society that believes that its own suffering must be passed on to others so that it will not be in vain is a society that will never advance. But instead, remain in a conservative bubble and will be quite content to remain there.

The American Revolutionary War also brought a new notion to the American social contract—private property. Now, private property is not unique to the United States. Other countries have private property. However, American private property is unique. Mainly being that the American private property arose out of the end of the notion of the feudal system, where everyone lived and worked on someone else's land. Instead, American private property is not just the notion of "this book is mine" or "I live in my very own apartment." But rather came the notion of "I own my own land and will defend it from all my foes, even if that is the federal government." Through that came the notion of individualism, and the American idea that the individual is constantly waging war with the collective.

Yet there were problems with this philosophy. Mainly being unnatural. Humans evolved to live in collective groups. All our closest animal species work together in groups.

This, of course, brings up the one thing that Americans, despite not wanting to hear, need to hear, even if the international community has to stage an intervention and slap them across the face. We live in a society. And because of that, we live in a collective, and we must start to act like it. The effects of the American culture psyche refusing to accept this can be felt all over the place. From people saying that Obamacare would result in government death-panels to people refusing to wear a mask.

There are a few reasons as to why the American cultural mentality is so vehemently against the notion of collective society. I will explain other reasons in later chapters. But one of them is the idea of the "self-made man." That one individual, through nothing but hard work and determination, managed to go from rags to riches. Another tokenization story that Americans use to stifle any criticism. Even though it is one story in a population of over three hundred million people, quite literally one in a million.

However, the notion of the self-made man truly falls apart. Whether we like to admit it or not, we live in a society. The only way for the self-made man analogy to work is if the individual starts off with literally nothing, lives in the middle of woods, gets absolutely no help from anybody, and from there, manages to rise to the top. Obviously, this isn't what happened. People get benefits from good schools, growing up in good middle-class homes, going to college, and etc. And thus, didn't make it on their own, thereby defeating the self-made man myth. In addition, just as how one can commit acts of evil in the name of God, so too can one commit acts of evil in the name of being a self-made man, for how else could the Sackler family or Johnson and Johnson get away with their role in orchestrating the opioid crisis if they didn't just claim they were self-made men and the American people in a very Pavlov dog fashion just roll over and say, "They're self-made men! They must be benevolent! It's not evil if they do it! For America to improve, it must immediately discard the notion of the self-made man and see it for the lie that it really is.

Through that comes the most evident example of government-private property clash—taxes. I have often heard from Americans that the reason as to why Europeans don't mind giving more in taxes to their government is because they are fundamentally lazy and don't value hard work. It is obvious to me, upon hearing this, that they never once ever met a German. For the German culture is one that promotes hard work and competition so much that the German economic theory, ordoliberalism, emphasizes the need for the state to ensure that the free market produces results close to its theoretical potential. Developed by Ludwig Erhart and later, expanded upon by men like Willy Brandt and Helmut Schmidt, it helped bring back the postwar German economic "miracle on the Rhine." Germany, as a result, has never lost a manufacturing job to outsourcing or even automation and was the first to recover from the 2008 crash. And has weathered the coronavirus economic fallout better than most.

Supposedly, free market loving Americans should admire the German system and be clamoring their representatives to adopt it. Or perhaps, Americans aren't really pro-free market competition at all. Yet despite this pro-hard work, pro-free market attitude, Germany has universal healthcare, strong labor unions, legalized prostitution, and tuition-free universities, all of which are, of course, paid for through taxes. How could supposedly free market loving, hard-work loving people be supportive of these supposed socialist policies? What's more, how could Angela Merkel, the leader of the Conservative Party, go along with these supposed socialist policies? Quite simple. The German people understand that they are part of the collective, that true-individualism doesn't exist, that they were benefited by a system. Therefore, they must pay back into that system. For the fundamental lesson that Americans need to learn is this: once you make it to the top, you have to make sure that other people get the same opportunities you had. Otherwise, it will look as though you got a free ride. Ironically, the supposed "if you want it, work for it" libertarians, when push comes to shove, will demand that everything will be done by charity or other volunteer work. To which they, I assume, will not be one of the volunteers; thereby, being the lazy people they accuse others of being of.

Ultimately, this inability to recognize upon Americans that they live in a society, that they are obligated to live under a social contract, that they are, in the end, part of a larger collective body of civilization has deadly consequences. The widespread coronavirus infections and coronavirus deaths are the most immediate consequences. But even beyond that was a disaster in the making. Under our current health-care system, hospitals that don't generate enough money are forced to close down due to lack of demand. This is particularly true in rural areas and low-income (mostly, minority) urban communities, where there is a severe hospital shortage.

As a result, many hospitals in the United States have had to contend with a huge stretch of resources in this pandemic due to overdemand. But who predicted this would happen? Bernie Sanders predicted this would happen. People who advocated for a national health service, like in the United Kingdom, predicted this would happen. Yet Americans were delusional by the notion of "government bad, get off my lawn." That they were willing to let such an inefficient system continue and for an excess amount of deaths to go on in order to appease their cultural mindset. If WWII were to happen today, the lack of Americans to engage with their collective obligations and fear of "government-takeover" would have meant that the United States would have been overrun by the Nazis in a span of five minutes.

This, too, provides a window into the future. For what has been experienced as a consequence of the coronavirus pandemic is only a glimpse into the next big battle—climate change. The fight against climate change would require large-scale mobilization by both the state and by the people of a kind not seen in the world since the Second World War. Large-scale rationing of meat and beef, nighttime blackouts, gasoline shortages, energy shortages on a scale not seen since the Three-Day Week in Britain, a ban on long-distance air travel, and rationing of foreign imports such as chocolate from the Ivory Coast or Vanilla from Madagascar. As well as the nationalization of all the oil fields, coal fields, natural gas fields, power plants, and the conversion of them into carbon-neutral sources of energy such as algae biofuels, and installing solar plants, wind turbines, geothermal energy. And the instillation of several carbon capture machines in order to make the United States a carbon-negative country, a status only Bhutan has. In addition, a green foreign policy would need to be implemented, making other countries implement the same green energy plans. And have the entire world connection by one green transglobal power grid, similar to the vast network of cables that lie under the ocean floor. Efforts that would surely require the disbandment of rugged individualism and the mass mobilization of the collective as a whole.

This mentality clearly shows itself in something that I had mentioned before, race relations. If we were to take the American social structure of Puritan colonial society, from a religious devotion to a higher power to hard work to repent for being a natural-born sinner, the glorification of suffering and hardship, what do we get? We get slavery, one of the darkest chapters in American history. But of course, it no longer exists. And by rebelling against the institution of slavery, African-Americans rebelled against the American social contract. Something that would make them traitors to the white Anglo-Saxon protestant elite or to anyone else who abided to the American social contract.

But since this cultural mentality is invasive, rugged individualism and rejection of the social contract is not limited to the right-wing. The neoliberal will claim that they are the true champions of all, but is that true? Indeed, neoliberalism may claim to be the counterweight to fascism.

But it will only speak out against social injustice so long as it does not threaten the coziness of their elitist racist suburban social structure. They will support immigrants from far-right rhetoric yet will not do anything to address the income disparity. They are pro-choice but will do nothing to address period poverty or the state of women's prisons. They say that the solution to everything is to have more minorities everywhere, or implement affirmative action, because it allows them to feel good about their status and not leave the confines of their couch. For they will cheer on people like Kamala Harris, ignoring the serious controversies of Kamala Harris record as attorney general of California. Ultimately, just the notion of her being a Black woman is enough to substitute her shady record with bullshit notions of "girl power," reminding me of Eric Andre's response to the question "Do you think Margaret Thatcher had girl power?" For them, those issues are irrelevant since they did not affect the suburban way of life. Indeed, they will claim to not be right-wing, but when push comes to shove, will devolve into right-wing elitists and care more about "triggering the rose twitter leftists" and make the Bernie Bros cry again than anything else. Indeed, if I were to go to the neoliberal corner of social media and see them engaging with communists or other leftists on issues of capitalism or US foreign policy, would I find them looking at their beliefs with a critical eye and questioning their own beliefs? A "I can see where they are coming from in regards to x, y, z"? Or will it just instead be the same old reactionary circle jerk of "Look at this dumb tankie tweet they said! Oh yes, we are so much more civilized!" As if it takes a Harvard education to take down Max Blumenthal.

However, even those who claim to leave neoliberalism and join groups like *Antifa,* more often than not, still cling to the old Pilgrim-era social structures. The most blatant example of this that I have heard of is the new trend of "land acknowledgement" or "I acknowledge that I live on stolen land." For it is the left-wing alternative of the time-honored American tradition of appearing to do something without actually doing anything. For acknowledging doesn't magically erase the problems of rampant alcoholism in Native American communities or the rampant poverty and lack of social services of things as simple as a supermarket or the missing and murdered Native American women.

Indeed, the left-wing argument of the "vote Democrat to save the minorities" crowd is very much an example of rugged individualism. For no one is going to simply drop whatever it is that he or she is doing and ignore whatever problems they have in their lives, unless they are speaking from an elitist class.

One thing I have noticed about a lot of modern American activists that come from a more neoliberal background or even a left-wing background is that, for them, nothing is of note unless they can intersect it with other issues. Everything and anything must be a racial justice issue. Homeless people, not my issue; homeless trans people, we must fight to end homelessness? Don't frame climate change as an environmental catastrophe; frame it as white supremacy! One must wonder, if this is the message of these "champions of the homeless" that they will only pick and choose in whichever direction the wind of intersectionality blows, how offended must homeless people truly be. Truly showing off their status as being a member of an elitist class.

Instead, it exists for the same reason that neoliberals champion more minorities in positions of power, to make people feel good about themselves rather than fix any of the actual problems. Even then, when push comes to shove, while the formal neoliberals turned *Antifa* acknowledge systemic racism, they still cheer when more minorities are in positions of power, even if they don't actually change anything. For surely, the average *Antifa* supporter must come to terms with why the most religiously devoted to being anti-racist are all white. The ones who engage in the most statue toppling are white. Is it really about being anti-racist or just making yourself feel good to cover up for a vehemently racist past that they don't want to acknowledge and rather suppress? Much like how the most anti-gay pastors turn out to be closeted homosexuals. While they acknowledge systemic racism and that solving this is bigger than the individual, they will still say that it is up to you, the individual, to change yourself. Harking back to the old Pilgrim beliefs that we are all born sinners, and we must work every day of our lives to repent. Belief systems that *Antifa* claims to want to abolish. We also can't ignore that *Antifa* has a very Americocentric way of looking at the world, ultimately coming from the same social flaws that enabled American supremacist attitudes in the first place such as, say, looking at the entirety of the Arab-Israeli conflict through the prism of modern-day American race relations. The number one thing I hear from European friends of mine when asked if "What message would you like to send to Americans?" is almost always "Please stop applying your racial paradigms here. They don't apply here. They never did."

When I see *Antifa,* I am immediately reminded of what George Orwell said in the road to Wigan Pier:

> *The first thing that must strike any outside observer*
> *is that Socialism, in its developed form, is a theory*
> *confined entirely to the middle classes. The typical*

Socialist is not, as tremulous old ladies imagine, a ferocious-looking working man with greasy over-alls and a raucous voice. He is either a youthful snob-Bolshevik who in five years' time will quite probably have made a wealthy marriage and been converted to Roman Catholicism; or, still more typically, a prim little man with a white-collar job, usually a secret teetotaler and often with vegetarian leanings, with a history of Nonconformity behind him, and, above all, with a social position which he has no intention of forfeiting. This last type is surprisingly common in Socialist parties of every shade; it has perhaps been taken over en bloc from the old Liberal Party.

Take the issue of redlining and gentrification. Despite all the calls to end racist zoning laws and end gentrification, they still choose to live in their all-white, gentrified, and high-cost luxury homes. Has one member of *Antifa* gone to the inner cities as I have? Or coal country as I have? Have they ever set foot in Youngstown, Ohio, or Gary, Indiana? Do they really stand for the working class as they claim to? Then, why don't they leave the cozy cocoons or their urban yuppie lifestyle, not unlike the neo-liberals who will not leave the cocoons of their suburban yuppie lifestyle?

Orwell later follows it up with this:

To this you have got to add the ugly fact that most middle-class Socialists, while theoretically pining for a class-less society, cling like glue to their miserable fragments of social prestige. I remember my sensations of horror on first attending an I.L.P. branch meeting in London. (It might have been rather different in the North, where the bourgeoisie are less thickly scattered.) Are these mingy little beasts, I thought, the champions of the working class? For every person there, male and female, bore the worst stigmata of snobbish middle-class superiority. If a real working man, a miner dirty from the pit, for instance, had suddenly walked into their midst, they would have been embarrassed, angry, and disgusted; some, I should think, would have fled holding their noses. You can see the same tendency in Socialist literature, which, even when it is not openly written de haut en bos, is always completely removed from the working class in idiom and manner of thought.

The Coles, Webbs, Stracheys, etc., are not exactly proletarian writers. It is doubtful whether anything describable as proletarian literature now exists—even the Daily Worker is written in standard South English—but a good music-hall comedian comes nearer to producing it than any Socialist writer I can think of. As for the technical jargon of the Communists, it is as far removed from the common speech as the language of a mathematical textbook. I remember hearing a professional Communist speaker address a working-class audience. His speech was the usual bookish stuff, full of long sentences and parentheses and 'Notwithstanding' and 'Be that as it may,' besides the usual jargon of 'ideology' and 'class-consciousness' and 'proletarian solidarity' and all the rest of it. After him a Lancashire working man got up and spoke to the crowd in their own broad lingo. There was not much doubt which of the two was nearer to his audience, but I do not suppose for a moment that the Lancashire working man was an orthodox Communist.

They, like the evangelicals, speak in tongues, spells, and backward Latin in a vague, half-asleep, semicoherent rant about white supremacy and imperialism and capitalism and collective liberation. But very rarely, if ever discuss the issues of people they claim to fight for—decline of the rust belt, the addiction and opioids crises, the homeless crisis, healthcare disparity, and etc. The kinds that, at any workers march, wave the Palestinian flag. As to when Palestine became the symbol of the working class, I never got the memo. And the fact that the ruling Palestinian Fatah Party is a member of the Socialist International should prove that no one should take the Socialist International seriously. For if they had not called themselves Nazis but instead the national socialist German workers party, I am confident they would be a member of the Socialist International. Indeed, while they think they are championing for the people, they are not changing the fundamental flaws of the American social contract. Something that the people left behind in the rust belt can tell and call out for its bullshit. The socialists that will win back the working class are the ones that declare themselves in solidarity with the workers and not in solidarity with the oppressed.

So in the course of the chapter, I explained what America needs to do to fix its social woes: abolish the self-made man and recognize your role in a collective. But this, of course, will get an immediate response of "but my freedom." Which brings up the other fundamental flaw in American cultural psychology: the concept of freedom.

CHAPTER 5

On the Concept of Freedom

This Independence Day is yours, not mine. You may rejoice, and I must mourn.

—Frederick Douglass

Freedom is the most stated word in the American vocabulary. It is also the most abused and the most misunderstood. Therefore, to understand freedom, we must understand the various types of freedom. Freedom to, freedom of, and freedom from, in addition to individual freedom and collective freedom. After all, what is freedom really?

There is first the notion of freedom to. I have the freedom to do something. It is the most common form of freedom expressed in the American psyche because it fits most with the rugged individualism that defines America. Therefore, it is the only one that Americans are allowed to possess. But as the American notion of rugged individualism is unnatural so is this particular form of freedom.

I am reminded of a video uploaded to YouTube by the right-wing YouTube Channel PragerU, who, despite its name, is not an actual university. And because it does not back up its opinions with evidence, is a disgrace to the academic profession and therefore, should not be taken seriously by anyone. The video in question was called "The War on Cars" in which the presenter describes the push to get more Americans off cars as "a push to destroy what cars represent: freedom." This, of course, was immediately met with backlash. Let's use the train as an example. A train arrives only on a fixed schedule and only stops at scheduled locations. Yet there is also the lack of traffic, the severely reduced threat of being delayed, and because you are not driving the vehicle, you are free to think about other things such as reading, eating, resting, and etc. How is it then that in a car, the supposed symbol of freedom and liberty, you are bound to the tyranny of traffic and rush hour stress?

Which brings up a more important question, are there fundamental flaws in the way that the notion of individual freedom is structured? Indeed, there is. For the reason why people feel more free in a state of collective freedom than in a state of individual freedom is because in a state of collective freedom, people are more inclined to the consent of others, and thus, democracy prevails. In a state of individuality, you are not required to care about the consent of others and thus, are not obligated to hold a vote. For individual freedom basically states that everyone is free to be his or her own tyrant, a sentence which basically sums up Thomas Jefferson's philosophy to a tee. To put it bluntly, if you encourage everyone to have the freedom to be as much of an asshole as they want, don't be surprised if you end up with a lot of assholes. So to answer the question of why Ayn Rand's ideals were so instantly accepted in America yet so laughed at elsewhere, the answer is simple: Thomas Jefferson was the original Ayn Rand.

When also discussing freedom and freedom to and freedom from, I bring an example—the French system of secularism, *Laicite,* where the French citizen is freed from religion by the state. In America, in many places, it is legal to have faith-based medicine and engage in gay conversion therapy. In France, both these measures will land you in jail. When discussing freedom, whose freedom is one referring to?

American notions of individual freedom are usually brought up within the context of a counterbalance to the powers of the state. But as I explained in the last chapter, sometimes a person with more power than you, that doesn't come from the state, will come along and threaten you. And you will need a higher power to act on your behalf, in this case, the government. This, of course, brings up a fundamental question with warnings about government power. This is not to say to be terrified of those who warn of government power but do so within the context of running for office on a platform of warnings of government power. After all, if you are elected on a platform of "government doesn't work," once in office, you will actively try to make sure the government doesn't work so that you can turn around and say, "See, I told you government doesn't work!"

Indeed, every single United States president who ran on anti-government platform expanded the power of the government. From Thomas Jefferson dispatching the navy to wage war on the Barbary Pirates without congressional approval to Andrew Jackson overruling the Supreme Court's rejection of the Indian Removal Act to Ronald Reagan unilaterally firing striking air traffic control workers. Government is not in and of itself sentient. Government is only as good as the people in it.

In it, notions of freedom must also be put into context with something very closely associated with freedom, although they are not the same thing—democracy. The idea of one person, one vote. While we associate democracy with voting for representatives, democracy can be applied to other objects. Nor is there one form of democracy. Switzerland, for example, is a direct democracy, where power is directly invested into the hands of the people. And so is, for example, labor unions or worker-owned co-operates or residential-owned apartment co-ops, a pinnacle of libertarian socialist thinking. Yet Americans, despite claiming to love the institution of democracy, will vehemently be against expanding democracy to other sectors of life. If you claim to support democratic representation in government but not in the workplace, do you really support democracy? Or instead believe Alexander Hamilton, who called democracy "the great disease?"

Indeed, it would not surprise me if demagogues immediately reject democracy and embrace dictatorship by saying that democracy is communism, much like how the segregationists opposing the civil rights movement said that race mixing is communism. Americans will begin to call to abolish democracy and replace it with—the free market. The slogan for this new campaign will be, "Save us from socialism, abolish democracy." After all, did anyone honestly believe that bombarding the American people with the rhetoric of "whatever the communists do, we do the opposite" would not create a generation, indeed, an entire culture of reactionaries without the ability to possess critical thinking?

I, therefore, come to the notion of collective and guaranteed freedom. There is this notion in American culture that you are not born entitled to anything. Yet this is immediately debunked by another thing that Americans also like to bring up: the Bill of Rights, a document that says that all Americans are (in theory) guaranteed with certain rights by the government. Freedom of speech, freedom of religion, freedom to refuse soldiers quarter, freedom from unwarranted search and seizures, freedom to remain silent, freedom to have a trial by jury, freedom to sue, freedom to have a lawyer acting on your defense, freedom from cruel and unusual punishments, freedom to have private property, and etc.

These rights are rights that Americans *are* entitled to, that one can point to and say, "My rights as an American that are constitutionally guaranteed to me by the government are not being upheld or worse, being violated." And if these rights are guaranteed by the government to all its people, although they are framed in the context of individual rights, are they also not collective rights? And thus, what about a collective bill of rights? Along the lines of FDR's second bill of rights, delivered in his fireside chat on the state of the union on January 11, 1944, where he calls for:

> *The right to a useful and remunerative job in the industries or shops or farms or mines of the nation; The right to earn enough to provide adequate food and clothing and recreation; The right of every farmer to raise and sell his products at a return which will give him and his family a decent living; The right of every businessman, large and small, to trade in an atmosphere of freedom from unfair competition and domination by monopolies at home or abroad; The right of every family to a decent home; The right to adequate medical care and the opportunity to achieve and enjoy good health; The right to adequate protection from the economic fears of old age, sickness, accident, and unemployment; The right to a good education.*

Is this bill of rights any more or less a series of guaranteed rights than the one written by James Madison? Indeed, if the Second Bill of Rights is something that has to be "earned" through toil, then so, too, is the first. And I would not find myself surprised if Americans start to say that no one is entitled to, say, Sixth Amendment protections of the right to a defense attorney. If you can't afford a lawyer, too bad, go out and get a job. Even though the constitution requires the state to provide people with a defense attorney, should they not be able to afford one.

Americans claim to love freedom, yet more often than not, the choice of individual expression is so often curtailed. Take the suburbs for example. I have mentioned them before in previous chapters. They are, more often than not, a drain on budgets. They wreak havoc on the environment. And they reinforce racial and class segregation. If costs of living in the suburbs were honest, no one could afford to live there. Yet the image of the suburbs is still forced on us. I have never seen a real estate ad advertising public housing. Commercials still show well-manicured lawn neighborhoods. Indeed, the elitist racist culture of the suburbs has manifested itself in the form of NIMBYs (Not in My Backyards), where now the only housing plots that are built are high-end luxury, with heavy government subsidies. Meanwhile, many inner-city neighborhoods remain empty and derelict, yet no one from the suburbs wants to risk venturing into neighborhoods with "undesirables." Indeed, it is very obvious that the government has a desire to enforce a certain lifestyle on its populace.

Through this, of course, we get into the freedom of persecution by the state. In which, the United States government has a long history of suppression. For what does the United States, the Soviet Union, and Nazi Germany all have in common? All three were founded on ideas. From America's democratic frontiersman of deep religious faith and appreciation of hard work to the Soviet Union being founded on Marxist ideas to Nazi Germany being founded on nationalist socialist Aryan supremacist ideals. Nation-states that are founded on ideas will do everything in their power to make sure those supposed ideas are upheld, even if it comes at the expense of suppressing dissidents. This is true even of supposedly liberal democracies like the United States, where to maintain liberal institutions, suppress all thought who call for a new direction. Thus, the ouroboros once again comes back to bite its own tail.

For the United States, to maintain its ideas of a liberal democracy, a long history of state suppression of dissidents has been maintained. One immediately comes to mind—the Comstock laws, which made illegal; anything deemed "morally obscene" from being sent in the mail which included on that list: socialist literature, feminist literature, and anything promoting gay rights. Another event that comes to my mind would be the mass arrest of dissidents opposing US involvement in the First World War. Or that all immigrants had to vow to turn become an anarchist or a socialist. Or even the Battle of Blair Mountain, where the US actively waged war on striking coal miners. Earlier, I had mentioned the lavender scare, where the FBI waged an all-out war on homosexuals. Actively accusing them of being communist infiltrators and working for the mafia, one of many things that led to the Stonewall Riots of 1969. In addition, the FBI engaged in unconstitutional wiretapping of anyone advocating for civil rights, gay rights, socialists, and etc.

The US claims to be a beacon for freedom of expression. Yet the *patriotic* act with its warrantless surveillance is still there. Furthermore, one thing that I remember from the Hillary 2016 supporters was their complete willingness to disregard evidence pointing to Hillary Clinton's corruption from Wikileaks. This is not to say that Julian Assange is a great man; the man has many flaws and did a lot of his actions under very shady circumstances. Yet the reaction that was given to Wikileaks, making them allies with the open lunatics of Mike Huckabee and Sarah Palin who called for Edward Snowden and Julian Assange's execution (which would have been unconstitutional, I might add), made me wonder, if these people were alive in 1971, what would they have said about Daniel Ellsberg and the Pentagon Papers?

Here, we must bring about neoliberalism and the Obama administration. For Barack Obama was new to many. He came to power in a time of turmoil, with a country suffering from the ravages of war and recession. He was the first Black president in American history. And he had appealed to youth voters like no other American president had before. He appealed to the young people, who was their president, like Ronald Reagan was to the boomer generation. And like Reagan before him, the generation would go out of their way to defend Obama, much like how Ronald Reagan was able to get off the hook for the Iran-Contra Affair.

Such as when it was revealed that many opposition figures in the Arab Spring that Obama was supporting had strong jihadist links. Culminating in the rise of the Islamic State popping up in Iraq, Syria, Yemen, Libya, West Africa, Somalia, the Philippines, and now Mozambique. Or when it was later revealed that the drone program used in Afghanistan had a civilian casualty rate of over 90 percent, a result of Obama expanding the Bush drone war after making a campaign pledge to shut it down. Or when the WikiLeaks revealed that the Obama administration was stuffing into his cabinet, Citigroup hedge fund managers. As well as continuing Bush's war on whistleblowers after promising to grant clemency, if not an outright pardon, to whistleblowers. As well as that Obama was instituting mass deportations and that the "immigrant cages" that became associated with Trump were started under Obama. And yet not only was Obama let off the hook, he, like Reagan, is highly praised, in spite of all this evidence mounted against him. The response I always get when people are pressed about this is "But he displayed a gay pride flag!" How insulting to the gay community that must be to use their history of struggling for equality and acceptance as a cloak to whitewash the bad elements of Obama's presidency.

And at the end of the day, if Obama was such a great president, then why was Donald Trump his successor? And if it was because "he was Black," then why did people who voted for Obama twice voted for Trump? And to those who say that they "did not know who was best for them," who are you to look down on people? For this attitude only reinforces the failures of neoliberalism. Despite claiming to be anti-elitist, neoliberals still cling to social elitist attitudes.

Through this, another fundamental flaw with American social structure—the media. I am reminded of a quote by Kuwaiti dissident Sami Abdullatif Al-Nesf, where he said, "The media acts like a mirror. If you take it to green pastures with water, it will reflect it. If you take it to a garbage dump, it will reflect it." Yet American media does not rank as top quality. Despite supposedly believing in freedom of the press, America does not rank number one in freedom of the press. After all, no media that believed in freedom of the press would have gone after Wikileaks in 2016. Rather, they would have gone after Hillary Clinton and Barack Obama or cover up a story about Jeffery Epstein prior to his death, as a bombshell report that did not get the attention it deserved found that ABC did exactly that. And that many media outlets won't cover foreign policy unless they concern US interests. Did any US media outlet except for the PBS NewsHour mention anything about the war between Armenia and Azerbaijan?

The failure of American media relies on another failure of American culture that I have mentioned before—the religious push to privatization. As a result of this, the American people have been contempt with something as important as delivering the news fall into the hands of a for-profit businessman, who will see the news is reported not fairly but to ensure the maximization of their profit. Such as the fact that Amazon CEO Jeff Bezos bought the *Washington Post* to become his own personal media outlet, and thus, "Democracy dies in Darkness." Or the fact that CNN news segments are laid out almost like a dinner menu—"Prime Time with Chris Cuomo," *The Lead with Jake Tapper, The Situation Room with Wolf Blitzer,* the news is not a dinner menu that you can selectively pick and choose, yet it is a phenomenon that I see on their cable counterparts at CNBC, MSNBC, and FOX. With all of this, is it no wonder that America's ranking for how free its press is has been dropping?

The push for privatization also poses another threat to freedom, true freedom—corruption. Americans will claim to detect corruption. But what is corruption, ultimately, but the privatization of government? If someone in government is bribed to do favors for a private corporation, that is the government getting privatized. Lobbying is essentially the privatization of government. After all, if wealth is power, then absolute wealth corrupts absolutely.

Here, I must draw upon a historical analogy. Americans are often taught about fascism through the rise of Nazi Germany. Yet the rise of fascist Italy is a more potent example of fascism because it was centered around the gradual conditioning of the violent, thuggish nature of Mussolini's red shirts and their slogan, *Me Ne Frego* (I don't care). That said, "They're fascists. Of course, they will beat people up, *me ne frego.*" So that when Mussolini appeared before the Italian people and admitted responsibility for the beatings, they gave him full dictatorial power because *Me Ne Frego*. Yet despite the end of Italian fascism, the spirit of *Me Ne Frego* has not died. It is manifested itself in America, of an elitist suburban class curious about the rise of anti-establishment movements who want to end corrupt politicians and primary prominent politics. Such as Alexandria Ocasio-Cortez's primary win over Joe Crowley. The number four Democrat in the House, with a puzzled, "What do you mean? They're politicians. Of course, they take big money. That's just they're nature." And the spirit of *Me Ne Frego* continues, a gradual conditioning of acceptance of corruption, hardship, crackdown on whistleblowers, etc., and a gradual eroding of democratic institutions.

For now that I have discussed the concept of freedom, the response will now be that it is not within the spirit of 1776. Which brings us to the sixth and final segment of this book: the Revolutionary Nature of the American Revolution.

CHAPTER 6

On the Revolutionary Nature of the American Revolution

But what do we mean by the American Revolution?
Do we mean the American war?

—John Adams

The American Revolution is the epoch of American history. Every year, on any occasion, the spirit of 1776 is invoked. As such, we must examine the American Revolution more thoroughly.

Now, I am not going to analyze the American Revolution from the perspective of more recent historians, such as the 1619 Project. Mainly because I think that teaching history from an activism standpoint is bad history. However, we must understand what the American Revolution was and what it wasn't.

It is often portrayed in American history textbooks that the American Revolution was fought to free America from the yoke of tyranny by an imperialist Britain. However, notions of British imperial tyranny make people come to mind atrocities undertaken by the British in India, Africa, and Ireland, not the United States. For Britain did not engage in mass plundering of wealth in America, as it did in India, or cause mass famine, as it did in Ireland, or instill sectarian violence as a means of divide and rule, as it did in Africa. Where was the tyranny? Where was the yoke of oppression?

The reason why this is relevant is because American false notions of tyranny have its effects on American politics. My mind immediately comes to former *Fox News* anchor, Chris Reagan, finally realizing that Bernie Sanders did not want to make America like Venezuela. But instead of doing in honest investigation on Denmark and of Scandinavia, it's pros and cons, she uses it as an opportunity to attack Denmark. To which everyone in Denmark saw and proceeded to laugh. When I had the opportunity to visit Denmark, the prime minister at the time was Lars Løkke Rasmussen of the liberal center-right agrarian-based Venstre party, so clearly, someone who would not support Bernie Sanders. Yet the country still has universal healthcare, tuition free college, high minimum wage, and strong labor unions.

This begs the question: why does no one in Europe scream "This is Communism! This is a tyrannical government takeover!" But such legacies are frequent in America? The answer is very simple. Because of geographical isolationism and an uninterrupted liberal republican form of government with no form of government to compare it to, the American people don't know what communism and tyranny are. Therefore, don't know what they aren't. Even during the colonial period, the power of the king was limited in the colonies. They largely governed themselves, and Britain, by this time, had a prime minister while Americans are often told of King Geroge III. How many Americans know of Frederick North, Lord North, second Earl of Guilford?

Compare this to Europe, where after thousands upon thousands of years of history, with different forms of government, from empires to kingdoms to feudal states to constitutional monarchies to parliamentary republics to communist police states and fascist regimes. Because Europe experienced communism, it knows what communism is, and therefore, it knows what it isn't. Because it knows what government takeover is, it knows what it isn't. Indeed, it is perhaps the truth that a constitutional monarchy with a monarch has limited power. It is the best means of keeping a check and balance on tyranny. Because just the mere presence of a monarch, even if the monarch is only ceremonial, is enough to remind people of a time when the power of one man to execute someone or start a war on a whim, and thus reinforce to people what tyranny and oppression actually is. Perhaps Donald Trump's attempts to hold onto power will instill a check and balance onto the cultural psyche of Americans and make them finally understand what tyranny is and what it isn't.

One theory with this is also the beauty of a multiparty parliamentary system, where instead of voting for a person, you vote for a party. By voting for a party, you are forced to discuss policy positions, not charm and charisma like is so often discussed in the United States. And with a multiparty system, you have a broad range of political ideologies to examine and to compare it to, and so you know what ideas are and what they aren't. If anything, saying that something is communism is an insult to those who lived under communist rule.

In addition, there is an idea that is pervasive amongst Americans that the American Revolution's ideals were new. Yet many of the ideas in the Bill of Rights were inspired by the English Bill of Rights of 1689. Sweden had already undergone an "Age of Liberty," which began after the Swedish defeat in the Great Northern War of 1700–1721 and lasted until Gustav III became king in 1771. During these fifty years, Sweden adopted a parliament and increased civil rights. What, then, was fundamentally new about the American Revolution?

In addition, revolutions have the problem of what happens the day after the revolution. For once you overthrow the ruling government, what happens then? In addition, a revolution must ask the question of who led it? Was it a bottom-up revolution of the masses? Or was it a top-down revolution of the elite? Was the revolution just a reshuffling of politics? Or was it a social revolution that completely transformed the social structure? One example of that is the French revolution, started by a group of people, angry with their king not caring about the massive impoverishment of the French masses, who responded with the storming of the Bastille and later, the Women's March on Versailles.

But there was also another group, the liberal enlightenment thinkers who wrote *The Declaration of the Rights of Man* and debated constitutional monarchy, republicanism, secularism, and etc. Except these two groups were not the same people. The people who debated the philosophical ideas of government never had to worry about where their next meal was coming from. And the people who stormed the Bastille were too poor and too hungry to care about what liberalism was. As a result, many liberal institutions became more and more disconnected from the masses, and thus, liberalism came back to bite its own tail. The Liberal Democrats in the UK, for example, must come to terms with why it was that the last time they were in power was during David Lloyd Geroge, over one hundred years ago.

My big bread and butter was always foreign policy. And through that, I have noticed a familiar yet very disturbing trend. Virtually, all online commentators who discuss foreign policy are European. You will find little to no American online commentators discussing foreign policy. And this should be seen as a giant red flag. It is not that Americans are not interested in foreign policy, as the anti-war movement has demonstrated, but rather they simply do not have the luxury to think about such things; since Europeans have the luxury of a strong social safety net. And because the Americans continue to act as their main defense force, they can afford to focus on other things. But the American suffering from food insecurity, home insecurity, and healthcare insecurity, will not care about things like the liberal world order, Fukuyama versus Huntingdon, is American retreat allowing China to fill in the void, and etc. Nor is this even fundamentally necessary; despite the fact that it is routinely banged into our heads that Russia and China are about to attack the west and overtake the west. Both countries are overdue for a major demographic collapse, significantly overblowing the threat Russia and China actually pose, much to the objection of greedy Europeans who expect the United States to continue to be their defense force for eternity.

The same thing can be found in the American Revolution. While there were genuine uprisings of disgruntled masses, such as the Boston Tea Party and the War of the Regulation, the people who signed the Declaration of Independence and drafted the Constitution were not those people, and if anything, were completely disconnected from them. And because of that, while the political structure changed from an autonomous self-governing series of colonial republics under the wider vassalage of a constitutional monarchy to an independent liberal Presidential Republican system, the social structure never changed. Because the French Revolution and the Revolutions of 1848 were popular uprisings, they transformed European social structures. Revolutions that transform social structures are not revolutions of a small elite but revolutions of the *vox populi*. Even as *Antifa* and other left-wing activists show a fundamental disregard for what liberalism is and what liberalism isn't, as well as the various schools of liberalism, ranging from classical liberalism to social liberalism, liberal socialism, utilitarianism, georgism, neoliberalism, liberal-conservatism, and etc.

Indeed, this is the fundamental flaw with not just top-down revolutions but also with great man history. Great man history is almost always a lie, a personality cult. In order to be a "great man," one must earn it. Earn it by transforming societies. So the question then is, "Who throughout history has deserved that title, at least within the modern era?" Only two people I have found to be worthy of earning that title: Mustafa Kemal Attaturk and Lee Kuan Yew. Both leaders radically transformed their countries in a direction that radically transformed them. Whether it would be Mustafa Kemal changing Turkey from an Islamic theocracy to a modern Western one, or Lee Kuan Yew transforming Singapore from a poor outpost on the brink of tearing itself apart over racial tension to a thriving multicultural Asian Giant. As much as Americans like to portray their founders as God-like creatures, none of them transformed their country and society like Mustafa Kemal Ataturk and Lee Kuan Yew did to theirs.

In addition, as America was born out of revolution, American culture is drawn toward seemingly revolutionary actions around the world. However, this opens a fundamental flaw in American understandings of revolutions. My mind immediately goes to the famous movie intro, "This film is dedicated to the brave mujahideen fighters of Afghanistan." The truth is, revolutions and other separatist movements are, more often than not, not motivated by resistance to tyrannical oppression but instead selfishness. Is Scottish nationalism really about fighting English oppression, or because they don't want to share oil wealth with the rest of the United Kingdom?

I mentioned before Obama's support of Arab Spring protests, even though it was widely known that many of them had jihadist links. A sort of "This film is dedicated to the brave anti-Gaddafi freedom fighters of Libya." Nor is this immune from the left. For as it, too, was a revolutionary ideology, a leftist version of Thucydides's Trap is put into place, a "This film is dedicated to the brave Houthi freedom fighters of Yemen." Are all ideas supposedly revolutionary good ideas? Was Thomas Jefferson's idea of a "natural law" and "natural rights" a good idea? After all, what is and what isn't a natural law? How do we know what rights are natural and which ones aren't? For once we know what things are and what they aren't, society can begin to move forward.

CONCLUSION

When the American people look at you (JFK) they see what they want to be; when they look at me, they see what they are.

—Richard Nixon

Throughout this manifesto, I have explained to you the problems with American culture and what is needed to change. To summarize, Americans must reject rugged individualism and embrace the social contract, acknowledge the fact that they live in a society, and reject all Puritan views and language of what hard work is and isn't. Reject all religious devotion to the free market and to notions of private property. Americans must acknowledge and accept the role of government and what government is, what freedom is and isn't, what tyranny is and isn't, and disband the idea of "American exceptionalism." In essence, Americans must put an end to "suburban culture" and "capitalist culture."

Not, though, when I say put an end to suburban culture, I do not mean an end to the notion of the suburbs. When I say put an end to capitalist culture, I do not mean put an end to capitalism. Capitalism is an institution that has been around longer than the United States was a country. America is not the only country that has suburbs, and suburbs already existed before the creation of "suburban culture," which only goes back to the 1950s. So when I say "suburban culture," to be more specific, I mean "Levittown culture." For America to live, Levittown must die.

And likewise, the same can be said of "capitalist culture." Take the videos coming out of the pandemic of people hogging toilet paper, some even selling it to others at a higher price. Americans tend to look at such things with horror and disgust. Now, replace toilet paper with houses. A man buys up all the houses and sells it to others for a higher price. Is the man viewed by the American media and the American public as a hoarder and look on with the same horror and disgust? Far from it, instead the man is viewed as a brilliant businessman, a savvy investor, and gets a spot-on *Forbes* magazine. Any honest man must look at the contradiction and udder one big, fat "go fuck yourself" to *Forbes* Magazine. This is capitalist culture. This is what must die.

But how?

Before I say how, I must say how not. America doesn't need a political revolution, it needs a cultural revolution. Yet in order to achieve the cultural revolution, we must take lessons from the country that implemented a full-scale *cultural revolution*—China. For if one is serious about implementing a cultural revolution, one must not implement what China did. For what China implemented was not a cultural revolution, it was a personality cult disguised as a cultural revolution. Instead, this revolution must be a revolution not of the state but of the common masses. Americans looking to implement radical reform must also not follow the trap of the French, implementing a reign of terror. It is very easy to overthrow an institution, but it's a lot harder to replace it with something else. Indeed, the fear of it repeating must never be allowed to become corrupted, such as the Second Punic War, the fear of another Hannibal invading Italy, and destroying the Roman countryside made Rome adopt a more offensive strategy. Enabling corrupt, powerful individuals to conquer lands on their own accords for the sole purpose of enriching themselves, leading to the eventual downfall of the Republic.

Nor will I expect it to a peaceful cultural awakening. Undoubtedly, there will be mass riots and demonstrations on both sides, for people calling for cultural change and those looking to preserve the old. But a new culture must emerge, and it must not be of the same fundamental mentality that led before it.

The reason why I like to bring it back to the planning of towns and cities is because they, more often than not, are a representation of the cultural values that society believes and what values they hope to instill in the next generation. The reason why European and American cities are so different is because their cultural values are different. European cities were built out of a feudal social structure, where American cities were built out of the notion of individual property rights. And we see it, too, in the results these social structures produce. If you built a town/city where people continuously interact with each other and everything is within walking distance, you will create a society of people that depend on each other, on a community. And thus, create a culture of social harmony, sustainability, and respect and concern for the democratic opinions of the majority. Likewise, if you build a town/city where everyone has their own individual allotment and no one has to interact, you will create a society of individualism, selfishness, and near-perpetual civil unrest.

Before I go any further, I would like to add that I do not mean all suburban dwellings, but I do mean the postwar suburbia that defines the American notion of the suburbs—the Levittown suburbs, with their cul-de-sacs, townhouses, single-family zoning, shopping malls, and etc.

Indeed, the suburbs represent the big mirage that is American culture. So much so that the famous moment of two St. Louis suburban whites pointing a gun at Black protestors should have forced the conversation about the racist, elitist truth about the suburbs. Alas, it didn't. The mirage can be felt in every element of the suburbs. I have mentioned before how the suburbs are a drain of money. For if you were to add up the infrastructure cost, cost of having to drive everywhere, and etc., it becomes rather obvious rather quickly that the idea of "low-cost suburban housing" or "working-class suburbs" is exposed for being the oxymoron that it is.

So then, why, if the suburbs are so bad in everything, do Americans cling to them like glue? The answer is relatively simple. To the American cultural psyche, it is their perfect Goldilocks, the perfect blend of individualism, of property rights, of Thomas Jefferson's ideal agrarian utopia, and all the lies and mirages that come with American utopia. So much so that when people called for revitalizing the cities, they did not do so by building new community centers but by building new sports stadiums, aquariums, shopping malls; in effect, suburbanizing the city. But it didn't work, because the suburban model they based it off of doesn't work. Even many of the new building of apartments is flawed because many of these new apartments are only inhabited by homogeneous, elitist suburbanites who do not interact and integrate with the community in which they belong to. Thereby, not improving the problems that culminated in the Long Hot Summer of 1967. In fact, in many respects, I would argue that the problem is being made worse.

But now, we must get to how it is that culture will be changed.

America has experienced much unrest over its history, particularly recently. But these protests follow a very similar pattern. There is a large nationwide movement, it lasts for up to several weeks even, but then, things calm down and everyone goes home. Thereby, not really changing anything at all. What is, of course, needed is real mass demonstration that can grind a society for months on end. These sorts of things have happened before. After all, what was it about a simple price increase on the Santiago metro that made Chileans change their constitution? What was it about a man setting himself on fire that made Tunisians oust their dictators? What was it about a rape that made Rome become a republic?

Such demonstrations of the masses must be made in order to achieve such a thing. But it must also coincide with a break from old ways of thinking. We are slowly seeing that in America, a nation that is becoming not just less religious but becoming more like Europe in that it is increasing a nation less of private property owners and more a nation of renters. Thereby, ending private property culture, a fundamental staple of American culture since the beginning.

I hope that reading this has fundamentally altered your perception of America, and that you, the reader, will take what I said to heart. So long and thanks for all the fish.